CONTENTS

THE DANGERS OF A SUPERNATURAL LIFESTYLE: How Procrastination Kills Prophetic Pioneers

EDDIE MASSEY III

ISBN-13: 978-0-578-51631-8

0 A CONFESSION FILLED INTRODUCTION

I have a confession to make. I should have finished this book a long time ago. Every morning, I get up early before the rush of the day, and I pray for quite a while. I wait in the presence of the Lord calmly. As random thoughts rush and rage through my mind, I simply still myself in God's presence. Instead of fighting the thoughts, I simply begin to give thanks to God. I thank Him for his mercy, and I let Him know how weak I am and how strong He is. As my focus turns toward Jesus, the distracting thoughts cease without me realizing it. Suddenly, God interrupts my praise or my stillness and begins to quicken me. In the blink of an eye, I arrive in a supernatural domain where God speaks to me. In this place, the Holy Spirit tells me about myself, those around me, and even the dealings of nations. He gives me many instructions, and unfortunately, I haven't followed them all swiftly. I've done far less than what the Father has shown me. I typically write down as much as I can remember about what God shows me and tells me along with the date and time. In my reflection this year, I've seen how procrastination will leave you full of vision with no fruit.

The Lord told me in prayer to write this book early in 2017. I worked on the project on and off, but I allowed myself to be blinded by busyness. Toward the middle of 2018, the Lord reminded me of what He told me to do and rebuked me for my disobedience.

He showed me how when we miss out on what He tells us to do, we place others in danger. Procrastination kills. There are so many people praying for answers and looking for hope. God responds by speaking to someone to manifest and be the answer to the prayer. The problem is that many of us really don't regard what God says as much as we think that we do. Procrastinators hold up God's ability to respond. As my Pastor, Dr. Shane Wall, often says, "God isn't going to jump off of His throne and do anything." God always uses people to advance His agenda on Earth.

As I've assessed my behavior and allowed the Lord to deal with me, I can see that by living according to the spirit of procrastination, I've held up Heaven's agenda in my life. So over the past six months, I've been making every effort to abandon procrastination. My repentance doesn't occur by me simply saying, "Lord forgive me," but by me choosing to aggressively divorce the spirit of procrastination. I've been completing unfinished projects and placing myself in position for divine alignment.

In changing and becoming a new man, I learned several reasons behind why I became a constant procrastinator. I always put off little things, like checking my mail, and other simple tasks that I could complete immediately. As I practiced unfaithfulness with little, I walked in unfaithfulness with bigger projects that the Lord commanded me to do. If we constantly practice procrastination, we'll procrastinate when it really counts. We like to imagine that we'll magically behave differently when the stakes are bigger, but that's not the case. Jesus told us plainly in Luke 16:10, "One who is faithful in a very little is also faithful in much, and one who is dishonest in a very little is also dishonest in much." We can't have more until we learn to manage little well. By procrastinating with little assignments God gives us, we set ourselves up to procrastinate the purpose that He gave us.

God has given each of us a purpose and that purpose is time sensitive. If we rebel against the time we were created for by delaying assignments, we will miss our purpose. A careful look at Joseph's life in the Book of Genesis shows us the importance of time. God created Joseph not simply to deal with the famine in Egypt, but to prolong the lives of the patriarchs of Israel who carried the seed of the Messiah. If there was no Joseph to receive instructions from the Lord in famine, the lineage of the messianic line could have died of hunger. Because of the obedience of Joseph and others who helped preserve the line, the words of the prophets of old were fulfilled in the life of our Savior, Jesus Christ the Righteous.

Often we don't have the sense of urgency that our purpose requires. We don't realize that, just as the faithful men and women of the Old Testament, our obedience is attached to salvation and deliverance. What God instructs us to do provides answers not only to our prayers but also to the prayers of others. From Genesis to Revelation, God has always used people to move His plans forward. Our obedience to God can affect what manifests on Earth.

In this book, I endeavor to uncover the hidden manifestations of the spirit of procrastination while giving you some practical ways to deal with the way that the spirit of procrastination manifests in your life. I will present the problem and give solutions. Oddly enough, most procrastinators aren't really lazy. They just allow things to get in the way of fulfilling their purpose in a timely manner. I hope that from my missteps you can learn not to let anything get in the way of what God created you for.

1 THE STAGNANT AND THEIR FEAR

To be honest, watching my grandmother's health gradually deteriorate over time was more difficult than her passing. Seeing someone so strong become so weak was something I had trouble coping with. She was filled with wisdom and understanding. She had a sweet voice that could calm the winds of a hurricane.

She would help at the drop of a dime. Her character was impeccable in public and private. I had the privilege of living with her as a little boy. She introduced me to the Lord and taught me to pray and read my Bible. If it weren't for what she imparted to me as a little child, I probably wouldn't be writing this book now.

Her health problems started much later in life. She tried to hide them the best she could. Her warrior heart wouldn't want anyone else's to worry about her. She began to fall occasionally more often, but then eventually it became too frequent to hide.

I remember one time she was walking down the hallway, and she just collapsed. My mother screamed and ran to her aid. The cat was out of the bag. We knew then that, despite how much she said everything was fine, there was something wrong.

The doctor told us that my grandmother had water on her brain. A condition where brain fluid isn't properly absorbed and builds up over time. The condition was causing her falling spells and short term memory loss.

The doctors did a procedure where they placed a shunt in her head to drain the excess water. Everything was successful, but it seemed like after that nothing was the same. Not too long after that, my grandmother developed Alzheimer's and eventually, dementia

She couldn't remember much of anything. A force of stability not just for me, but my whole family became unpredictable. Sometimes she remembered us, other times she didn't. Often she thought she was back in New York where she grew up instead of the rural South.

When I would come by to visit, it would always be difficult to convince her that she was really at her house. Apparently, I looked like her brother because she would always call me by her brother's name, "Aubrey," and ask me to give her a ride home even though we were already at her house.

Seeing her gently fade away was difficult, especially with me being so young. In a sense, I felt like she was gone already even though she was still with me. It was something that only God could heal. Some in my family would say I distanced myself as I became older. But the distance was the only way I had learned to deal. They say you're only as old as your greatest trauma and when it came to my grandmother I was 10 for a while.

Despite the pain of losing her, I learned something from that experience. My grandmother loved the Lord, had a great diet, but still ended up with a disease. In fact, the doctors were astonished at my grandmother during that first visit.

Although she was in her late sixties or early seventies at the time, the doctor was amazed at the condition of her body. He said she had the body of a forty-year-old. I remember always hearing her juicing carrots and cucumbers every morning after her 4 am prayer time.

After staying with her for some years, I remember growing a bit weary with her cooking style. There was no salt or seasoning on anything. She was very intentional about how she ate, and to this day, I almost never add any salt to my food.

When it comes to health, people often focus on diet. Some say eat kosher, some say vegetarianism, and others prefer the Mediterranean diet. Regardless of the diet, the environment plays a role in our health. I believe that the environment doesn't just mean the pollutants in the air, but pollutants in the environment of the mind.

My grandmother had to go through a lot and had a difficult husband that caused high levels of stress. When illnesses come, they seem to attack the most vulnerable places. My grandmother's diet kept her body healthy, but the stress made the brain the prime target.

Stress can make the diet have no effect. Many of us in the body of Christ have superb spiritual diets. We go to powerful churches and eat the right food. We go home and study God's Word personally as we feast on His Truth. Our diets are impeccable, but we, like my grandmother, are stressed.

Most of us, however, are creating our own stress by disobedience. God gives us instructions and we sit on them. The Lord tells us about our character and we make no changes. The Holy Spirit gives us business ideas and ministry solutions that we never put into action. We have books that remain unwritten. Projects that have been incomplete for years.

We seem to have more unfulfilled prophecies than fulfilled ones because of our inability to follow through on the instructions God gives us. As we continue to walk with God, we get more and more revelation, correction, chastisement, and rebuke to take us into our future, but for some reason, we choose to remain the same.

The water of the Word sits on our mind instead of being absorbed into our being. We become puffed up with knowledge and revelation and filled with outward activity that produces rotten fruit. We become stressed by our lack of conformity to God's will.

We begin to be burdened by what's on our minds. The amount of unfinished projects, unfulfilled prophecies, and uncorrected character flaws begin to appear insurmountable.

As God's Word sits on our minds, we develop anxiety because of our inconsistency. The guilt of what we've left undone begins to weigh on us. We're overwhelmed because of all the unused Word.

The projects, the ideas, the proposals, the how and the why become the forefront of our internal conversations. Instead of letting the Word wash us with its refreshing water, we let it sit and become stale. So rather than walking on the water, we have water on the brain.

There are many reasons we don't allow God to complete the work that He started in us. We procrastinate, we get busy, we get tired, and we get plain lazy. To be honest, sometimes we just don't like what God says.

Whether through the preaching of the Word, personal prophecy, or one on one time with Jesus, God often gives us instructions that are uncomfortable. He always makes us do things that require a leap of faith.

He likes to give us commandments that produce sustainability and longevity while we often don't want to sacrifice instant gratification for God's timing. In many cases, the commandments that Jesus whispers in our ears require significant character and behavioral changes.

We hesitate on doing what Jesus tells us because we prefer the promises of God over the changes that He requires us to make. God's will always produces a journey in which He delivers us from significant character flaws and deadly coping mechanisms that we've used to survive without His help.

But, we must be honest. Hearing God's Word without transformation is senseless. After all, God is a supernatural being that gives us supernatural instructions in public and in private. There is no limit as to what is available to us in the Word of God. In today's World, we have an overflow of access to scripture, teaching, and revelation. We can pull out a Bible app and even watch sermons back to back on YouTube. We have a smorgasbord of divine power.

The old cliché rings true, "with great power comes great responsibility." When Jesus spoke to Peter and told him to walk on water, God imparted to him unprecedented power.

This age has been given a dimension of knowledge and revelation that has never been seen on the Earth. The Prophets of the Old Testament and the Apostles of the New Testament didn't even have complete Bible, let alone 24/7 access to sermons, books, blogs, and even Q&A websites. God's question to His church is what are we doing with the increased access?

"Truly, truly, I say to you, whoever believes in me will also do the works that I do; and greater works than these will he do, because I am going to the Father. -John 14:12

Do we see the greater works flowing through our lives on a daily basis? Do our lives look like all of the sermons that we watch? Jesus gave Peter a simple command, "come." Through that four letter word, Peter walked in a supernatural dimension that many yearn for, but aren't even close to accessing. Despite Peter's unparalleled opportunity, he still sank.

Although Peter was one of the 12, and Jesus was literally standing with him on the water, he couldn't stay afloat. What hindered him from maintaining authority over the molecules of H_2O? Water on his brain hindered him from walking on water. We can't walk on what we're not delivered from in our minds. It's safer to stay in the boat if we're going to be led by the elements of the environment and not the grace of Jesus Christ.

The harsh wind and strong waves are no place for people willing to step out, but unwilling to stay out. Peter fell because he didn't maximize the help he had in Jesus. If we are going to continue to hear these teachings, read these books, and receive this deep revelation from God, we have to put the truth into practice, or we will fall.

It's not that Jesus would be unable to catch us if we fall, but there comes a time where the burdens of disobedience make the thrust to fight for the future fall away. A lot of us are tired of fighting because we seem to keep falling. We won't let faith in Christ carry us all the way.

For it would have been better for them never to have known the way of righteousness than after knowing it to turn back from the holy commandment delivered to them. 22 What the true proverb says has happened to them: "The dog returns to its own vomit, and the sow, after washing herself, returns to wallow in the mire." -2 Peter 2:22

Peter was able to pen verse 22 with such wit because he learned the hard way. He eagerly stepped out and walked on water soon to fall and be rescued by Jesus who walked him back.

Peter knew the dangers of turning away after knowing the truth. He saw the mercy, grace, and hand of Jesus give him the grace to recover. Because of both his ambition and recovery, we don't have to become dogs that return to their own vomit.

Start your journey with Jesus on the water and stay with him as long as He's there. Don't step out of the boat and turn back because of the wind and the waves. You can hurt yourself if you turn back.

Peter's fall on the water was traumatic and scary, but Jesus didn't coddle him. As the Lord reaches His hand out to Peter, he rebukes saying, "O you of little faith, why did you doubt?"

Doubt in the biblical Greek, according to Helps Word studies, refers to "going two ways" and "shifting between positions." Peter was trying to live by what he saw with his eyes and what he knew in his spirit at the same time.

He knew that Jesus was Lord, but he also knew that men can't walk on water, especially in storms. We have to make a firm decision on where we get our knowledge from. Will God be our source, or will our experience alone govern our beliefs?

Peter became like the water he was walking on. The water vacillated and fluctuated based on the wind. Peter became like the water instead of the Christ as soon as he responded according to the wind. He took on the nature of what he was supposed to have authority over, so he began to sink. He walked in the realm of water instead of the realm of the immovable Christ.

Many of us are just like Peter. We're trying to live between two opinions at the same time. One of the manifestations of the dissonance between what we know to do and what we believe is possible comes in the form of procrastination. When God speaks to us, we hesitate and find ourselves sinking.

When then do we really procrastinate? What is the deepest root of our subtle, yet rebellious stance against Jesus? We pridefully procrastinate when God demands obedience that is attached to the possibility of suffering.

The mere sight of rapidly shifting weather patterns makes us afraid of the potential suffering on the other side of the wind. This mindset would be fine if we were only natural. But because we've accepted Christ, we have become the supernatural children of God.

God's seed is always supernatural, which means our fear of suffering isn't justified in His sight. His first-born endured the cross, so we should be able to handle the waters of the sea.

Procrastination is a sin that we like to overlook. It's not as sexy as coming against cancer or rebuking what some call a Jezebel spirit. In charismatic churches, people seem to have an affinity for coming against demons and principalities with their words alone.

I'm sure Satan's minions get a kick out of hearing

us pray, yell, and scream against demonic activity. They're unmoved because they know how undisciplined we actually are in private.

Demons consider us on their side. By not stepping into the waters that we're called to, we give evil the power and opportunity to wreak havoc on the lives of others. By avoiding our duty to Christ, we are complicit with the demonic activity that we pray against.

Supernatural authority does not come by praying, fasting, and speaking in tongues alone. God's authority is most effective in our lives when we're promptly obedient to His divine will and purpose.

The devil knows how many things that God has placed inside of us that we refuse to manifest because we prefer the comfort of procrastination over the rigor and suffering that comes from progress.

Our so-called spiritual warfare tactics are laughable at best when Jesus always operated in discipline. We have no authority over what we refuse to discipline in our own lives. We have a mindset that the only sins are the ones "they" do. They being those who we look down on.

We don't drink, smoke, curse, or fornicate, so we assume that we're in great standing with God. We must be careful not to allow ourselves to be blinded by the pride that can come from deliverance and transformation. Righteousness apart from the work on the cross is self-righteousness.

We've given God some of our issues, but there are areas, like procrastination, that we haven't fully submitted to Christ. We don't really see procrastination as a sin. The word sin in the biblical language refers to us missing the mark. According to Helps Word studies, it comes from the concept of an archer missing the target.

When we procrastinate on what God wants us to step into, we don't simply miss the target because we didn't know how to aim. We miss on purpose. We chose to hold back God's plan. We chose to give the enemy more time to keep us in bondage.

We miss the mark because we prefer to wait. Our preferential treatment of God's Word is a setup and mark for future bondage. For every area that we procrastinate there will be a degree of bondage.

We may not see what we're stuck in, but whatever area Christ doesn't have can't grow into maturity. The mature know how to grow because they are willing to handle suffering. We can avoid or delay suffering by procrastinating, but, consequently, we will also avoid the maturity required for our purpose.

By faith Moses, when he was come to years, refused to be called the son of Pharaoh's daughter; Choosing rather to suffer affliction with the people of God, than to enjoy the pleasures of sin for a season; Esteeming the reproach of

Christ greater riches than the treasures in Egypt: for he had respect unto the recompence of the reward. -Hebrews 11:25, KJV

Moses grew into a great Prophet by his willingness to suffer. God had a plan for him to be a mighty deliverer, but Moses didn't begin that way. After all, he was afraid to speak in front of Pharaoh because of his stuttering problem. Moses, however, was willing to suffer. Because of that, he grew into what God purposed for him from the very beginning.

No one arrives in purpose upon God calling them. There is a growth phase, and even upon arrival, there's more growing to do. In order to initiate and maintain God's growth plan for our lives, we must be willing to follow Christ to a bloody and painful cross. There is no crossless path to destiny, so there's no reason to procrastinate by looking for ways to avoid the cross.

What God says is going to seem scary and there are times where we will hurt. At the end of the day, by advancing into what Jesus says, we will look more like Him each passing day.

A Christ-like image is the purpose of life. We can't let our fear of people hearing us stutter and stammer hold back God's purpose. God's purpose in our lives is so much larger than our excuses for procrastinating.

Without Christ, there are more things against us than for us, but with Him, Romans 8:37 says, "We are more than conquerors." We often use this verse for comfort, but rarely tap into the power behind the full context.

36 As it is written, "For your sake we are being killed all the day long; we are regarded as sheep to be slaughtered." 37 No, in all these things we are more than conquerors through him who loved us. 38 For I am sure that neither death nor life, nor angels nor rulers, nor things present nor things to come, nor powers, 39 nor height nor depth, nor anything else in all creation, will be able to separate us from the love of God in Christ Jesus our Lord. -Romans 8:36-37

Although the Apostles were facing death daily, they prevailed. Even though they were battling the most vicious evils of their day and wrestling with the foremost principalities and demonic powers as they pressed to get the gospel out into the world, they conquered.

It is not what we do in comfort that makes us victorious. It is what we do in opposition that makes us conquerors. We can never say that we've applied these Holy Words to our lives if we've never faced obstacles and endured suffering.

To produce what God wants us to produce we must shun our fear of suffering and climb into the waters of destiny. But how then does one embrace such an unenjoyable thing like suffering?

...and when they had called in the apostles, they beat them and charged them not to speak in the name of Jesus, and let them go. 41 Then they left the presence of the council, rejoicing that they were counted worthy to suffer dishonor for the name. -Acts 5:40-41

Unlike the Apostles, we don't see suffering as a blessed opportunity. The only way to go through difficulty with power is to understand that every time God gives us an opportunity to suffer, we are being presented with a chance to look more like His Son. Looking more like the Son means we're deepening in intimacy with the Father.

For this reason, our greatest aim is Christ. We should share his pain tolerance, a tolerance that allows us to die to ourselves daily. When we are looking to be like Christ, procrastination, and every other ungodly habit or character flaw, begins to fall off.

If He is our constant aim and pursuit, darkness can't stay because the light of Christ will shine on and expose everything that is unlike Him. If we're pursuing Christ with all that we have then we will take on the mind of Christ as Philippians 2 tells us:

5 Have this mind among yourselves, which is yours in Christ Jesus, 6 who, though he was in the form of God, did not count equality with God a thing to be grasped, 7 but emptied himself, by taking the form of a servant, being born in the likeness of men. 8 And being found in human form, he humbled himself by becoming obedient to the point of death, even death on a cross. -Philippians 2:6-8

So often we quote verse five and omit the following verses that define the mind of Christ. To have the mind of Christ is to have a mind to be obedient to the point of death. We must humble ourselves and realize how honorable dying for God is.

When we die for God, resurrection is just around the corner. The suffering of what He calls us to do will only last for a while, but after three days He will raise us up.

Do you procrastinate regularly? If so, you're neglecting so many suffering opportunities that can bring you closer to Jesus. Don't ignore the Holy Spirit. Do what He tells you quickly so that you and the Son will be the spitting image of the Father of lights.

When we procrastinate regularly, we never build up the pain tolerances to handle the cross that God has called us to. Jesus was made for the cross on Calvary, to be the Lamb of God, and to take on the sins of the world.

As His disciples, we have also been made to take on a cross for a particular season and a particular time. If we hold back continually, we'll be comfortable with a counterfeit cross. In Luke 4, Satan tried to get Jesus to take a counterfeit path to purpose by taking a shortcut and bowing before him. If we continue to bow before the god of procrastination, we may receive the kingdoms of the Earth as the Devil promised Jesus, but we will never fulfill God's assignment for our lives. There is no crossless way to victory.

Jesus should be our aim. Every chance to suffer is great and precious. If we cherish our opportunities to grow by embracing the challenges of what God has called us to do, we will move past the wind and the waves of life, step out onto the water, and stick with the Lord.

2 THE COMFORTABLE AND THEIR BLIND SPOT

I spilled out every drawer in my office on my floor. Papers were everywhere. I literally couldn't believe it. I looked everywhere. I ransacked my car, my house, and everywhere in between. Every time I thought I saw a glimmer of hope in some envelope, it was quickly exterminated by a quite literal emptiness.

It wasn't in any binders. It didn't fall into any folders. I kept thinking to myself how stupid could I have been. How could I let this happen! Regret is one of the most painful emotions because you realize that there is nothing you can do to change what you've done. God often shows us the future, but He hasn't provided us a way to return to the past and change our decisions.

After I sobered my thoughts, I came to the disappointing reality that I had just lost a check for $5,000. I quickly shifted from regretting the past to reshaping my future. Something had to change. It wasn't my company, our initiatives, or my employees. It was me. I had known I was quite unorganized for a while, but it never really cost me this much. No pun intended. I had to change everything including how I saw myself, what I was capable of, and how I handled things.

By the grace of God, I recovered the check, but I knew God was giving me a wake up call. I don't only minister in my church. Part of my calling is also entrepreneurial. Through that, God uses me to reach people who normally have never heard the gospel, but my success in the business arena depended on my capacity to develop my greatest weakness- being organized.

This was an area I gave little effort to grow in. After all, I had a great excuse. I grew up in chaotic environments. Disorganization was the norm for me, and although I knew my habits weren't the best, I used where I came from to excuse myself from where God wanted to take me. Our upbringing and life circumstances do not excuse us from the call of Christ.

Although I had made changes in other areas, this one was holding me back from stepping into the fullness of what God spoke over my life. Over time, I placed more value in how I was than how Christ wanted me to be. Ultimately, I opened up the door to stagnancy.

Things weren't moving as fast as I thought they should, not because of my plan or vision, but because of the area that I refused to improve. My business and life grew a lot faster when I decided to stop settling for being unorganized. God moves quickly when we're ready to handle what He has for us. Stagnancy dies when we come alive to what Jesus has been telling us all along.

One of the major reasons that things go stale in our lives is because we grow stale as people. We get confused when our ministries and businesses don't grow. We're shocked when we see sinners outpace us in life and take on new territory.

We prophesy to people, and they move forward while we lag behind. It seems that so often we pour out so much, but reap so little. We pray and pray, but nothing seems to change. The problem is not what's happening around us. The problem is what we're not allowing to happen in us.

God's Word comes, but I've come to notice that few people truly change for the better according to the Word. A lot of people feel better and sound better, but few change for the better. Many of us reach a certain place in God and become comfortable in that level of closeness.

For some of us, we only want to be close enough to God to get what we want. It may be deliverance from a harmful habit. Others want to make more money. Some stay with God so they can find a spouse. Once God blesses us with what we really wanted, He doesn't hear from us anymore.

Others remain in fellowship with God, but they lose the fervor they once had. Often in charismatic churches, I see aspiring ministers pray and fast and seek God with intensity until they learn to prophesy. Once God begins to use them in the supernatural gifts of the spirit, or they get ordained, they begin to coast toward Jesus instead of running toward Him.

For most people, we change a lot when we first come to Jesus, but then there's something that He requires us to change or let go of and we don't want to. I believe the majority of believers are very similar to the rich young ruler found in the Gospels.

16 And behold, a man came up to him, saying, "Teacher, what good deed must I do to have eternal life?" 17 And he said to him, "Why do you ask me about what is good? There is only one who is good. If you would enter life, keep the commandments." 18 He said to him, "Which ones?" And Jesus said, "You shall not murder, You shall not commit adultery, You shall not steal, You shall not bear false witness, 19 Honor your father and mother, and, You shall love your neighbor as yourself." 20 The young man said to him, "All these I have kept. What do I still lack?" 21 Jesus said to him, "If you would be perfect, go, sell what you possess and give to the poor, and you will have treasure in heaven; and come, fol-low me." 22 When the young man heard this he went away sorrowful, for he had great possessions. (Matthew 19:16-22)

We're willing to give up certain habits and make many changes, but we're unwilling to give up the things that we value the most. So ultimately, we become stuck at our last breakthrough moment with Jesus. We're unwilling to give up the character flaw, sin or habit that we most value so we're no more powerful than our last deliverance session. Through lack of change, we develop poor character that is governed by the spirit of procrastination and not the Spirit of God.

The difference between most of us and the rich young ruler is that we stay around Jesus to keep our conscience clear. We still go to church, but we have a premeditated notion of what we're committed to addressing in our lives and the things that we stub-bornly refuse to let go of. Because our transform-ation is only as powerful as what we're willing to let go of, most of us actually haven't changed much.

By ignoring Jesus, we develop a prophetic blind spot as to why God hasn't done what He said He would do in our lives. As we ignore change often, we end up desensitizing ourselves to the changes necessary for our purpose. Willful ignorance has disastrous im-plications on the fulfillment of prophecy.

Prophecy is not fortune telling; it is expressing the

heart and will of God concerning the future. If we reject the change necessary to step into the promises of God, we reject the promises. It is time for God's people to arrive in the prophetic destinies that have been foretold and that takes daily reflection, evaluation, and change.

Many of us were raised in painful environments that did not cultivate who God called us to be. No matter what, our experiences pale in comparison to the transformative power of a loving Christ. The world was formed by the Word of God which means that God can rework us according to His Word. The devil has led us to believe that our habits and our identity are one. The devil has tricked many of us into believing that demonic strongholds and self-protection mechanisms are personality traits that come from God given identity.

I settled for thinking that I was just an unorganized person because that's how I had been my whole life, but that was a lie. So many of us would have bold new personalities if we would come out from the power of the devil's blind spot that keeps us in the bondage of stagnancy.

For every level of expansion, a new level of deliverance is required. God's ministry to us is to constantly deliver us from things that we didn't even know we needed deliverance from. Stagnancy is an evil thing that holds back destiny from coming forward and we must have no relationship with it.

As God delivers us, so-called personality traits break off and we begin to see who we really are. Some of us have fallen more in love with how we see ourselves than with God. Because of that, true deliverance can't be sustained. The rich young ruler had many possessions, but there was something I believe that he valued most of all- how people saw him.

He identified himself with his wealth. His greatest possession of all was how he was seen not what he had. If we want to have a different fate, we must throw away how we see ourselves and aggressively pursue looking like Christ every day. As we see from the gospels, we can't hold onto ourselves and follow Jesus at the same time. We must die.

There are practical ways that believers can come out of the quicksand of stagnation. We have to truly evaluate our lives according to what God has already told us. One thing that we should do often is to regularly review prophecies God has spoken and evaluate our character, temperament, and habits in reference to them. With regular reflection, we can prepare according to the future.

I remember listening to a sermon from a man of God where he noted that as a boy it was prophesied that he would be a preacher. From that moment, he began to prepare often studying the Bible 6-8 hours in a single day.

If we don't adapt the habits of our future, we won't be prepared when the season arrives. Are you select-ive in what you choose to be prompt about? Pro-crastinators aren't just late for meetings, but for the arrival in their destiny.

The spirit of procrastination has birthed a culture in the church that is casually carnal. Like casual drug users, casually carnal believers know how to do just enough procrastinating while avoiding en-grossment. We have found the habits necessary for the future optional because we prefer to endorse habits that compete against our purpose.

We've come to a place where we even find certain sins acceptable as long as we don't commit them all the time. With the habit of delaying our obedience we've mistreated and abused God's sovereign grace.

Because our views on sin are only moral, we refuse to acknowledge the chastisement of James 4:17.

Therefore, to him who knows to do good and does not do it, to him it is sin. -James 4:17

God doesn't simply want us delivered from the lying, gluttony, and fornication. He wants to see us move into the lifestyles that are conducive for our purpose. When we know that a change is necessary, but we are unwilling to commit to that change, we are in violation of the purpose that we've been cre-ated for.

Some of us, on the other hand, begin the process of changing habits, but we become arrested by the illusion of progress. We get comfortable with the fact that we started a new habit or that we changed for two weeks.

We'd rather be celebrated for victories that have not been tested than hunger for the longevity of God. To keep our change, we must surround ourselves with people and systems that will help support our movement into what Jesus has called us into.

The casually carnal Christian finds growth optional. The place of grace for them becomes a safe space to feed the ego. We get consumed with that concept that we're not who we used to be and begin to excuse ourselves from further personal and professional development.

The comfortable among us make excuses for lack of prayer time. We see spending personal private time in God's Word as optional. Many of us believe that attending church is enough, but serving is optional.

Therefore we complain about needs instead of addressing them. Our inaction allows stagnation to flow into God's plans. Those of us who are active instead deal with stark insecurities. Our service to God is then limited to soulish or carnal desires. In other words, we end up serving in a capacity that helps us feel better about ourselves. Ministry endeavors become a personal therapy for the soul instead of a duty to God to care for His beloved flock.

Above all the aforementioned issues that casual carnality causes, the greatest sign of its manifestation is when Holy Spirit inspired teaching does not bear fruit. Our lives should always mirror what God is teaching us through personal prayer and Bible study, our spiritual leaders and brothers and sisters

When God is speaking, but we're changeless that means we're casual. Some say that they are changing, but just at their own pace. While deliverance, transformation, and change do have a personal pace, we have a lot to do with how quick change comes.

The river of change can flow at the pace of our willingness. If we are to grow, we must first become frustrated with where we already are. Until we become uncomfortable, there will be no innovation. When we look at the history of the Earth, some of the greatest inventions and new technologies arrive at a time of constipation of resources.

In times of war, famine, political fallout, and disease outbreaks, the flow of resources are constrained and men and women must search for innovative solutions to new problems. Often they must find transformative solutions and reevaluate old problems so they can devise a more efficient means to address them.

In times of constipation, we get creative and find

ways to break barriers. There are seasons where God allows us to become spiritually constipated because it's time to be uncomfortable with where we are.

A great many of us have desensitized ourselves to the necessary frustrations of God by continually ignoring the Holy Spirit induced knowing that there's more in us.

If we're too comfortable with where we are in God, we will be unable to perceive the subtle nagging influence of the Holy Ghost saying, "There's more in you. Do more. Be more. Reach more."

Until we stop worshipping today's victories, we will be unable to cling to the promises of tomorrow. If we don't embrace uncomfortability, we will embrace stagnation. The stagnant live with their lives on autopilot.

When we're on autopilot everything we touch loses livelihood slowly. Every endeavor that God calls us to stagnates even to death. When something or someone stagnates they are gripped by the immortal quicksand of the enemy.

While a person, organization, project, or endeavor, may be dead to their purpose, they become alive to the devil. When we refuse to grow and lead people in a manner that consistently stifles growth, we give Satan the opportunity to advance his agenda.

Death has been the agenda of the thieving serpent

from the beginning.

The thief comes only to steal and kill and destroy. I came that they may have life and have it abundantly. -John 10:10

The deceiver often does not combat our present victories so that he can steal our hunger for more of God. He likes us to dwell in the nostalgia of the past. Satan loves when we become enamored with how God used us back in the day, and we don't notice that we're bearing less fruit today.

Once we're comfortable, we're full and hungry for nothing else. Once Satan has our hunger, we stop eating, which means that we can no longer grow. The hungry grow, but Tthe devil's master plan is suicide by starvation.

Once we're dead to God's plan, we give Satan legal right to destroy everyone and everything that we're assigned to by repeating the process among them. One of the most explosive attacks on the church has been the spirit of suicide.

In our blind spot of comfortability, we've believed that the spirit of suicide only manifests to make a person kill themselves. The spirit of suicide has a far deeper reaching agenda to reach.

When suicide comes, it's not coming after a person, but a purpose. There are people walking the Earth right now who don't even think about killing themselves, but they're making every effort to kill their ability to walk in purpose.

The manifestation of suicide comes in the form of self-destructive habits. Suicide tells us to go back to our old mess and embrace what we know is our kryptonite. Suicide isn't just among the depressed and faint of heart; it's working among healthy and happy people who are blindly avoiding the enjoying their freedom from the full magnitude of what God has spoken over their lives.

When we avoid what God has called us to do, we can't see the spirit of suicide lurking in the corner grinning at our irrelevancy. The enemy wants nothing more than for us to be immobilized in the reason that God placed us in the world.

Jesus can never send someone who's unwilling to move. When we let go of where we are, we can see the future more clearly. We must be willing to shun the tempting waters of procrastination and rise above the tide. God is uttering from Heaven to His people, "There's more in you that I want to do." There are sudden breakthrough moments available to His people who are willing to arise.

If we don't arise, the minions of the enemy will hold the people that we're called to become in bondage. A major reason that people don't want more is that they're afraid of losing it all.

A love for the present level has diluted our love for God and our love for obedience. We're afraid that if we go bigger, say more, or do more that we will comprise what we've already done. The delusions of the devil have made us forget Jesus' warning to us.

Whoever seeks to preserve his life will lose it, but whoever loses his life will keep it. -Luke 17:23

If we don't let go of what we've built in the present, we have no route to obtaining God's rewards in the future. If we rid ourselves of selfish notions of ministry for notoriety and fame, we'd realize that there's more in us.

The future is for those who are willing to move in the motion of Christ and not in the stagnancy of the devil. God is laying out strategic disruptions in the Earth that will fill the hearts of men and women with surprise blessings and opportunities. The only way to tap into the manifestation of God's plan is to rid ourselves of our own plan. We must surrender our lives to truly live the lives that we want to live. Without God, we won't grow. If we don't grow, we can't plant and harvest the nations. Will you surrender?

The pleasure of the current level does not compare to the rewards of the next. If we spend our lives casually dispensing the drug of carnality, we'll always neglect our blind spot. The fact of the matter is that no drug user tries a drug with the intention of becoming an addict. Procrastination is a strong drug and there are no casual users.

If we allow what's in our blind spot to delay our change we will be trapped in hopeless cycles of knowing that we have more, but not doing more.

3 THE ANXIOUS AND THEIR PAIN

There was no reason to believe that God had deserted me, but that's how I felt. When I came back home from college, my mom and I didn't have much. My dad had passed away the previous year, and we had to make ends meet.

It can be hard finding a job in a rural town if you majored in Applied Mathematics and Computer Science. Every job offer I got was too far from home and, after my father's death, there was a dire need to stay home to support my family. Our house was on the verge of repossession and I was just stuck.

Growing up in poverty, I had gone through far worse in my life, but I always had faith in God and He always came through. However, there was something different about this time in my life. I suppose college had jaded me. The stark realities of the world became more real to me than God's Word. In this moment of my life, the childhood faith I had was inoperable.

For the first time, I was hopeless. It really wasn't about the money, the home, or the job. What really ate at me was uncertainty in my relationship with God. I wasn't really sure if God was with me. Had he forgiven me for my past mistakes? Was I being punished for something I had done?

I couldn't care less about the lack in my life, but the lack of clarity was destroying me on the inside. I became utterly depressed so I would just sleep my pain away. When I would wake up, I could feel this intense heaviness on my chest and I would quickly be reminded that everything was the same.

Even when I was out and about, I could feel this negative feeling in the pit of my stomach that I can never really describe. As my mental and emotional state deteriorated, so did my health.

I began to deal with sudden nausea, vomiting, and fatigue. Typical of that time in my life, I slept to take away my sorrow. Little did I know this time when I laid my head down, God was about to say something that would change everything.

I had a dream where the Lord spoke to me and said, "I'm not going to pity you. You'll either trust me, or I'm going to leave you in this season twice as long." When I woke up, I was astonished.

I knew I had a decision to make. I could either think the same and see the same results or change my mindset and reap new results. From that moment on, I recommitted my heart to trusting Jesus and knowing that God was with me no matter what.

I quickly gave up my anxious thinking and I relinquished my right to worry. The cloud lifted and my body began to adjust to restored freedom in my soul. Mind you, nothing about my situation changed that day but me.

Some weeks later, I went to play soccer and had a lot of fun. Afterwards, an older gentleman and I struck up a conversation. Turns out he was a research professor working on a NASA project and he was looking for someone with a Computer Science background. That became a remote job for me for the next few years.

The job helped me to take care of the pile of bills at home, and on top of that, a friend donated a car to me. When my heart changed, I saw God's hand change. God could have given me those blessings much earlier, but He had a bigger plan.

He didn't want to bless me with a self-destructive mindset. I would have been unable to hold what He wanted me to handle. When my mind was in alignment with Him, His blessings began to effortlessly flow.

One of the tactics the enemy uses against those of us who decide to put on the full armor of God and walk in the supernatural lifestyle is to question us out of our peace. We have peace not from what we have, but from Who we have.

If we permit him, the devil will make us question our security blanket with Jesus. He will make us feel that we're not forgiven. He'll make us feel that our circumstances dictate God's approval or love for us. He'll make us question our reality.

When the devil gets us to question the power of the shed blood of Jesus Christ flowing through our lives, he's opening the door to insanity. If we're willing to question the nature of Christ's forgiveness in our lives, we'll be willing to question everything else that comes from our relationship with Him.

Peter began to sink because he started to question whether Jesus could keep him above water. He heard the winds and the waves which made him unsure if he could be upheld by the Savior that first called him to stand.

The seed of doubt produces the fruit of hesitation, fear, anxiety, depression, and a host of other debilitating issues. Peter's doubt may have caused him to fall into the Sea of Galilee, but many of us fall into the sea of depression, sickness, backsliding, and even suicide after we doubt God.

Some of us minister and do many mighty works for God, but on the inside the devil has us trapped. If my story is any indication, there are some illnesses that we're dealing with in the body of Christ that won't go away by dietary changes or casting out demons.

They're physical manifestations of mental health disturbances. The health of the mind affects the health of the body. Some people have been asking God to heal them for so long, not realizing that physical health is available at the moment they allow mental clarity to manifest.

It's almost like jumping off of a roof and asking God to heal the broken leg. Then when Jesus heals us, we go and jump off the same roof again but we blame God for our injury.

Some people receive physical healing from Jesus and then go back to the same worry, stress, and anxiety that caused the ailment in the first place. These mental disorders are causing other areas of our lives to be disjointed.

For some, thoughts of doubt and fear don't seem to cross over into physical manifestations. Instead, these spirits stir a hatred for life and believers are pounded by suicidal thoughts.

Feeling unwanted by God and unforgiven creates an unbearable pressure that some no longer want to experience. The devil has tricked us into thinking that the best way to alleviate the pressure of feeling undervalued is the cessation of life.

When we take hope in the literal fact that Jesus gave His life for us, we can remember that there's no need to take our own. We don't have to sink down into a place that is irrecoverable.

However, some of us, would never even consider taking our own lives to cope with the pain that comes with doubt. Backsliding, isolation, and secret sin on the other hand appear to be more suitable alternatives.

The devil twists the things of God so that they feel like a weighty pressure. So many believers are worried about whether they are pleasing God or not. Instead of asking God where we are with him or seeking counsel from a spiritual leader, we allow the spirit of condemnation to drown us in doubt which ultimately leads us into a backslidden state.

I used sleep as a coping mechanism, but others, even in the body of Christ turn to drugs and alcohol to temporarily escape from the pressures of reality. The devil would like for us to believe that taking an unholy vacation from God will give us the rest we need, but instead, the violent grips of addiction can become our portion.

When we step out of the boat and walk in faith, we must continue to proceed with faith because the dangers of our decision to step out can have dire consequences

We should never worry about whether God loves us or not. We should never wonder if God really forgives us or not. We must walk in faith according to what He said regardless of what we feel about ourselves.

Miracles don't require much from us, that's why they're miracles. Jesus simply asks us to give Him what we already have and He takes care of the multiplication process. The time we spend worrying opens the door once again for procrastination to manifest in our lives.

The time we spend thinking is the time we should be spending moving forward. Some of us are trapped in a never ending sea of despair and freedom can only come if we step out into the fullness of what the Father has spoken.

Mental and emotional pains engross us to focus on how we feel instead of what God told us to do. In reality, a lot of the pain we experience comes from neglect. We've been neglected by others and we also neglect our own interests.

We hurt to see others offended, but sometimes we become so immersed in the pain of others that we can't tell what's going on with ourselves. We become emotionally unstable, our moods shift often, and we gradually enter into long term depression, anxiety and suicidal tendencies.

Our culture of social media usage doesn't help the matter. We've become adapted to a digitized culture that glorifies superficial achievements on news feeds and fosters a destructive comparison mindset. We feel unaccomplished and unfulfilled because we don't have the latest car or house. Our security and self-esteem is shell shocked when we keep seeing people married and having babies, but we're not. When we're already unsatisfied with where we are in life, scrolling through social media can be like picking at a dire wound.

The pressures of life and the pains of anxiety get all the more overwhelming. We end up competing with people from across the world that we only know superficially. Some of us are depressed because we see the blessings of "friends" we follow but haven't spoken to since high school. A constant reminder of where we're not and what we don't have is depressing. For some, a digital detox is required.

A lot of our pain precedes our digital lives. Much of our pain is simply due to improper care. In our bodies, for example, we often take simple pains very lightly. When we have recurring headaches and migraines, we simply medicate ourselves instead of getting to the root cause of what's going on.

We wait until dramatic events occur to inquire for help. Acute pain can become chronic if left untreated. Ignoring the wrong pain can ultimately lead to a fatality. Many of our pains require immediate attention, but we become so accustomed to living with them, they remain unaddressed. Procrastination is veiled in the pains that we refuse to confront.

Just as our bodies need exercise, a healthy diet, clean water and air, our minds and hearts require a suitable environment to function properly. A great way to deal with pain is to talk with trustworthy friends, spiritual leaders, and even healthy therapy.

Pain can open the door to a procrastinatory way of life that limits our exposure to the good success that God has already claimed for us. When we're in pain, we slow down and lose our rhythm, but it's time to pick up the pace by getting the help that we need to move forward.

Dealing with unresolved hurt alone will leave us with nothing but our negative thoughts charged with the secret whispers of the devil coddling us in the fear of rejection and illogical worries of the past.

If we don't resolve our pain, we won't take charge of the purpose we've been given here on Earth. The only resolution to our pain is to be completely honest with God about where we are. Afterwards, He can pour out a level of healing where He visits our minds. Through that supernatural visitation, He'll miraculously deliver us from our memories and moments of defeat, victimization, word curses, and extreme traumas.

Through the support of our brothers and sisters, we can manage to cope with what hurts us. In the presence of Jesus, we can be totally healed from the hurts of the past.

The issue is when we feel like God is the source of our agony. Some of us actually hold unforgiveness in our hearts against Him. We feel disappointed by Him because of the things that He allowed to happen or because of unfulfilled promises. Now is the time to reconcile with the Father.

Our childlike disappointment in God has receded our ability to see Him as a safety net in trouble. We feel as if God owes us an apology for what's happened over the last several seasons. The trouble is that when we distance ourselves from intimacy with God, we lose sensitivity to what He's saying.

We can hear His warm, affirming, and soothing affirmations and corrections only if we let go of what we're holding against God and run to the secret place.

You make known to me the path of life; in your presence there is fullness of joy; at your right hand are pleasures forevermore. -Psalm 16:11

When we come to the presence of God, we can have deep joy even in the most uncertain moments. We must not neglect the fact that as disciples, there are some pains that are required for our purpose.

The bloody cross of Christ and its pains are our inheritance. We share in His cup as we die and experience death daily through situations that grow and also challenge our security in Him.

Walking with Jesus in pain reminds me of what I watched my wife endure during pregnancy. Her organs were shifting and making way for what was to come. The movement of her organs caused sudden, strange and unusual pains.

The fact of the matter is that we can't get mad at God because pregnancy is painful. Pain is a natural part of the process. When we're giving birth to purpose, He's not going to take away the pain of childbearing just because He loves us. Just like a pregnant woman, the organs of our soul must shift to make way for what God is birthing through us. There are necessary pains that we must endure to bring forth the promises of God in our lives.

Some of us are even like the baby in the fetal position. God has us in the womb being groomed and pain is carrying you into greatness.

Many of us were born into a culturally induced coma filled with trauma, envy and heavy pain. Our families didn't know how to orient us toward our purpose, but the pain that came from the under preparation is a part of what God is using to launch us. You're in the fetal position because you're about to be launched into a new level of fire. The fire of God will take hold of you, and people will want an encore of what your destiny has to offer. Prepare for your purpose regardless of the strain of the pain. Frustration is the context for your growth and development.

The pain of anxiety can be odd, unnerving and destructive. But God has some powerful constructive criticisms about how we handle pain.

Then Jesus told his disciples, "If anyone would come after me, let him deny himself and take up his cross and follow me. -Matthew 16:24

There is a necessary pain that leads to death in our walk with Christ. There are times where we are rejected, betrayed, offended, misused, and abused. If we don't manage pain well, we won't manage purpose well.

These same pains can constrict the forward motion in the future that God has called us to. There is a dimension of pain so intense that we can't even think clearly. Life is full of trauma; after all, there would be no need for armour if we weren't in a spiritual war.

How we handle the pains and disappointments in life will affect our ability to manage the wars of the future. The devil is deliberately planning attacks around our weak moments. He knows that we're too strong for his tactics when everything is going well, so he likes to use every resource to exact pain on our pressure points.

Our ability to handle pain is an earmark of Christian maturity. Christ didn't curse God because of the cross. He embraced the pain and endured the shame because of the hope for tomorrow.

If God permits a painful experience in our lives, He's also permitting a resurrection experience. The grave can't even hold a believer that is poised for purpose. Life after resurrection is always more powerful than after birth.

There's more authority, power dominion and authority after the grave. When we walk into what God has called us to, we walk into unprecedented power. The release of God sends us into difficult battles so that we can have power over what we come through.

A challenge in life is often a sign to what God wants to give us authority over. Challenges birth the promises of God. Pain births the promises of God. God wants to give His people new births, but the vehicle of the promise is pain.

We must renew our pain tolerances to handle the level of glory that God wants to bring us to. The people of God are poised for purpose and prominence can never be led by pain because God has to get the glory out of every situation.

Feelings are unpredictable and if we're led by them, our behaviors will be unpredictable. We should live lives consecrated even unto death, which means we must permit an opportunity for death to manifest in our lives.

There will be uncertainty, trials, troubles, and travails that strategically position us for the future. To avoid God ordained difficulty is to miss the mark of prominence that God has promised for His people.

4 THE BUSY AND THEIR CHRONIC DISTRACTIONS

As usual, that morning I woke up to the Lord showing me something. Sometimes I immediately understand the interpretation. Other times I have to figure it out later. One of the things He showed me this particular morning was very easy to understand.

Unfortunately what I saw wasn't in my favor. I had a contract to publish an online course, and I was far behind schedule. I had a vision when I woke up that morning that they were going to go in another direction.

When I checked my email, that vision that I had was confirmed. I lost the contract. Thousands of dollars plus royalties for a product that was a hot topic at the time gone in a flash.

This opportunity wasn't something I led myself to do. The company approached me and the Lord told me exactly how to create the course. He showed me a vision of the outline and even the financial dividends that he wanted me to make from it. But in my slackness, I let God's plans for me fall to the wayside.

During the time where I was refocusing myself to complete the course at the last minute, I came down with a heavy case of bronchitis. Every second I was coughing. Recording was absolutely impossible and set me back another six weeks.

If I would have moved when God initially spoke to me, I wouldn't have had any problems. The course would have been completed before I had even gotten ill.

I didn't really realize it at the time, but my problem was that I was a busy procrastinator. I had a lot on my plate at the time. I had a full-time job, and I was a full-time student. I was an Associate Pastor at my church and I also ran a non-profit that I founded. Not to mention, I was also planning a wedding to my beautiful wife and we were pressing a deadline towards home ownership.

In my wealth of busyness, I managed to excuse myself from coming up with a system to work on the course over time and thereby excusing myself from the blessings of God. We may have good excuses for why we don't attend to something God has given us, but our excuses won't grab the fruit for us.

Leaving God's instructions unattended to for a

given season, always leaves us underprepared for the next season. What we procrastinate on today, we will have to pray for tomorrow. Not too long after my contract was axed, I had an overflow of unexpected expenses arise.

I was very busy, I was making a lot of impact, but nothing in my life seemed to bear fruit at the level I really desired. Some would say that I had too much on my plate in that season, but today, I actually have more to manage. Back then, I had two major issues. I focused on how busy I was instead of how to best use my time. I also didn't know how to prioritize tasks.

Most people assume procrastinators are lazy and slack, but what I learned about myself and many others is that procrastinators are some of the hardest working people you will ever meet. I believe that many gifted and hardworking people are burdened with an array of responsibilities and the devil deceives them into putting important things on the backburner.

By the time we revisit the things that we placed on the backburner, they've crumbled. During that season of my life, the Holy Spirit rebuked me about how I manage the responsibilities that He placed under my care. He told me, "Whatever you don't give attention to will die."

Just like a plant that we don't water, death can come to whatever we neglect, even if God had a plan for it. If we don't water daily, there will be collateral damage.

The devil has deceived a lot of us into thinking that we're busier than we actually are. When God gives us something new to do, we seem to assume that we don't have the time to get it done. Of course we'd never say that to Him, but our actions speak for themselves.

Many of us constantly meditate on how busy we are. Some even wear it as a badge. Every day we decree and declare busyness into our lives. We spend so much time thinking about how busy we are that we can't discern how free we actually are.

We end up meditating more on how busy we are than the Word of God. Psalm 1 tells us to meditate on His Word day and night, but in our stress, we leave no space to think on the great riches and treasure of our salvation in Christ. This leads to depression, anxiety, and a lifestyle that tends toward the incomplete.

We venture to new goals and begin new projects out of doubt and guilt instead of the faith and fire of the Holy Ghost. Even worse, we take our fatigue into the ministries that God has called us to.

We have work, school, family, church, ministry, and so many things to balance that it seems very unfair for the Holy Spirit to add anything else to our plates. There have been several times where

I've prophesied to someone and they immediately began crying. You'd think I said something really heartwarming or a heartbreaking rebuke.

Instead, I let them know God's plan for their life and they saw it as a burden. "Another thing that I have to add to my schedule," they'd say.

For many, it was literally their dream, but they were heartbroken by that fact that God's plan would require steady and consistent discipline. They hoped that God would suddenly thrust them into the stage of purpose instead of building them into it.

We have become so overwhelmingly burdened by the non-essential cares of this world that God's plan for our lives seems like an extra responsibility. God gives us instructions to arrive at the moment of destiny that we've been created for.

To disobey Him is only to our demise even if we have to make personal, professional, or career sacrifices to do so. Prophetic people are well known on Earth for their revelatory acumen but known in Heaven for negligence.

People find it amazing that we can see far into the future, call out names, and unlock powerful mysteries and secrets from Heaven. Yet, the Holy Spirit is grieved by the fact that our revelation doesn't match our actions.

Many of us have Earth shattering global visions, which require high levels of discipline and focus, but we operate with inconsistent mentalities, habits, and patterns. We assume that because God has spoken to us, His Word will magically manifest regardless of our investment.

Our busyness does not excuse us from making the required investment into our purpose. A life centered on busyness and not on Christ will be an unfocused life. A distracted life is a life void of fulfilling divine purpose. Proverbs warns us about the dangerous results of being careless and lacking focus.

> *Whoever is slack in his work is a brother to him who destroys. -Proverbs 18:9*

To be slack in Proverbs 18:9 means to "let drop" or to "sink." If we allow busyness to be the reason why we allow areas of our lives to sink, we're being destructive. We can't be led by our schedules. We must submit our schedules to the direction of the Holy Ghost.

If not, the devil will throw unnecessary tasks in our way to distract us from what God has ultimately called us to do. Emotional distractions are a key strategy the devil uses to keep us from making time for our purpose.

When the Lord tells us something favorable about our future, our emotions are roused and we jump into action. We begin working immediately and we give all our energy into what the Lord spoke.

We become intently focused until the stir of emotions dissipates. As two weeks go by and the excitement wears off, we lull the Word of God to sleep. We don't feel it anymore. The calling that once gave us hope for tomorrow is buried under boredom. This behavior is what makes demons so bold today.

They're not afraid of prophetic people anymore because most of us have short attention spans. We don't finish our books, complete our degree programs, or maintain our businesses because we love to be excited, but renounce longevity.

We jump from project to project, book to book, business to business, and idea to idea. We work in this manner because we've become a generation led by what excites us and not by what pleases God. Many of us feel unfulfilled simply because we don't finish many of the things God assigns for us to do.

Pastors in particular often fall victim to this scheme of the enemy. In the modern era, successful pastors can't simply be great preachers anymore. They must be great leaders. In our tech-infused world, powerful prophetic teaching is accessible at the click of a button so a strong Word isn't enough to grow a church anymore.

A pastor's leadership capacity is what determines the size, depth, and breadth of a congregation. Some of the most profound teachers will continue to minister in store front churches because the devil sends distractions to hinder their leadership development and focus.

The hindrances to leadership growth trickle down in the members as the mere threat of resistance or difficulty becomes a signal to flee. Challenge now drains the people that the Bible calls "more than conquerors."

The devil's systematic attack on the expansion of God's Kingdom doesn't stop there.
. The enemy uses the tactic of internet and smartphone addiction to convince us that we don't have enough time. We complain about how rapidly time flies and how we can't find the time to manage everything God has given into our hands, but we don't invest our time wisely.

Instead of investing our time in activities that strengthen us for our purpose we frivolously waste it on Facebook, Snapchat, WeChat, and YouTube (feel free to insert your favorite time-draining social media platform here).

We claim that we don't have enough time, but a 2016 study from MediaKix, a social media influencer company, had some very alarming results. The average person will spend seven years and eight months of their life watching television. They will also spend five years and four months on social media.

Unfortunately, we're cultivating the same addictions for the next generation. A report from Common Sense Media shows that teens are spending around nine hours per day on social media.

Our proclivities have become the devil's doorway for the entrapment of our youth; his goal is for the next generation to have the same poor habits that we exemplify. . Some of us can't even work without a tab open for Facebook while we're on the clock. These dangerous addictions are gateway drugs for hardcore procrastination.

Many of us are investing in time in activities that will bring no dividends for our purpose. According to contemporary science, much of our social media habits are actually destroying our ability to focus and ravaging our mental health.

As we work on our business plans, we're also texting, scrolling through Facebook, playing music in the background, and watching a YouTube video. Stanford University Professor Clifford Nass who's done extensive research on our media multitasking says that we're "chronically distracted," have trouble "managing a working memory" and suggests that the research unanimously shows that people who chronically multitask are actually poor at multitasking.

The devil has systematically made us believe that we're busy all the time because of our high stress levels while keeping us distracted by whimsical musings on the internet and television.

While I don't believe that social media itself is evil, we've allowed it to rob God of time that belonged to Him. Then, we complain that we didn't have enough time to focus on what He told us.

We have become distracted beyond measure and my concern is that on judgement day, Jesus will look at our lives and the only thing that He will see is our Facebook news feed because that's where most of our time has gone.

We want to be like Joseph and make it to Pharaoh's palace, but we're unconcerned with what it takes to stay in the King's court.

Many people start churches, non-profits, and initiatives. Yet, how many remain after a single year? Many of the most profound prophetic people have the sight to begin something new but lack the hunger to pull on God for the supernatural keys to longevity.

One of the most dangerous characteristics of many busy people is the tendency to launch a smorgasbord of new endeavors without ever completing their prior assignments. This leads to a habit of constantly jumping from project to project without a firm focus.

There are many visionaries among us with far too many unfinished projects open. Much of this undeveloped fruit originates not only from poor planning, but a lack of empathy for people.

We have found ourselves in a place where we are ok with releasing half-written books while hosting conferences and trainings where we don't have the proper competency. We are not truly valuing the need to give people the nutrients that they need.

Ministerial ventures that flow in both church and secular arenas have become aggressively consumed with a focus on how to sustain income and not how to help people.

Without a love for souls, many of us are creating services and organizations that do not bear much fruit. Only when we have the care of Christ can God multiply our endeavors.

Some of us have busied ourselves to make us feel important. Even when the Lord does pour out ideas and visions for what He wants to be built on the Earth, we take His desire as our opportunity to increase our self-esteem. The entity then becomes self-driven, self-motivated, and insensitive to the movements and pressures of the Holy Spirit.

The busy are dangerously distracted by self. Being highly active helps us cover up pride, insecurities, fears, and inconsistencies instead of confronting them head on with God's love.

When there are so many self-driven assignments on our plates, we embrace another overlooked spirit-rushing.. As we jump from project to project, we want everything to be done quickly, so we rush.

Our hunger to arrive at completion overrides the Holy Spirit's passion to bring forth God's excellence in an endeavor. In the 21st century church, we'd rather be done than complete. We'd rather feel accomplished than be effective.

When we rush, we dilute effectiveness and erase power which leads to a prophetic warning from the book of Proverbs.

Haughty eyes and a proud heart, the lamp of the wicked, are sin. 5 The plans of the diligent lead surely to abundance, but everyone who is hasty comes only to poverty. - Proverbs 21:4-5

If we move in haste, we will bankrupt whatever we're producing. Even if we succeed in creating what we want, we will give way to poor management. Many movements, ministries, and businesses are impoverished in the realm of fruit because they began by fornicating with the spirit of haste.

The children of haste are governed by poverty. If we allow the rushed nature of humanity to plant a seed in what God has given us to do, we are shipwrecking its opportunity for growth and permanency.

Proverbs 21 also teaches us to combat our lust for completion with diligence. By building over time, with careful attention, millions can be made. Whether the fruit is financial, social, or spiritual, we can scale to a great magnitude when we apply diligence to what God has given us.

Diligence is not optional for abundance. There is no shortcut to do a great work in the Kingdom of God. Mega impact requires great focus and attention to detail. Without these traits, we will build structures that crumble with the tide, wind, and waves of change.

For some, the early signs of abundance have distracted us into casting off diligence. Premature success is a conqueror of great men and women. The habits we use to move into greatness are the same habits we must utilize to maintain greatness.

The seduction of rushing also comes into play with busy people because of the stress and strain of our daily schedules. We must develop consistent systems to evaluate our progress on our goals and projects.

They say Rome wasn't built in a day and I doubt Noah's ark was either. Regardless of how much we want to be done, we can't let a lust for the finish line trick us into the deadly distraction of rushing. The distracted die early.

Switching back and forth from work, school, ministry, and business endeavors can be mentally draining and stagnating without proper systemic support. The mismanagement of simple day to day tasks produces a buildup of life clutter.

Unopened mail, overdue bills, underprepared

meals, and filthy laundry are not only signs of poor management, but mental and spiritual clutter often produced from busyness. The magnitude of life clutter inebriates us, making getting major tasks out of the way impossible.

At the end of the day, the plethora of so many incomplete tasks makes us wait until the last minute to address them, and by the time we do, we've procrastinated ourselves into a brick wall. If we don't fix what's broken now, the consequences may be unacceptable or even catastrophic later on.

Thus we can say, our mismanagement leads to procrastination, and our procrastination to rushing, and our rushing to poverty.

To come out of poverty in any area, we must let go of the trigger to our procrastination. We must get to the root of how, when, and why we procrastinate to come out of the vicious cycle of poverty. Whether the root of our mismanagement is schedulistic structural, systemic, or cultural, poor habits can kill the future.

Our habits today are a window into what our future will look like. If we're mismanaging where we are now, we're telling God not to increase us or advance us because we're not ready for His more.

God gives more to those who are open and ready to receive more. Openness to God is not something we can prove with our lips, but only with our actions.

If we're open to His movement in our lives, we have to make room and let go of things that are taking up space.

There are many distractions in the lives of God's people that are occupying the spaces where blessings should be. Until we come to grips with the fact that two objects cannot occupy the same space, we will live on the same level and advance very little.

Our gift can make room for us and sit us at tables among great men and women, but our positive habits, informed by the Holy Ghost, will be what keeps us there. If we rush, procrastinate, or remain distracted, we'll look back and wonder how we missed the mark.

5 PROHETIC STRATEGIC PLANNING

I felt my heart ripping on the inside moment by moment. There was this deep unsettling feeling in the pit of my stomach because I knew that I had done wrong. I hate disobeying God, but I had really dishonored Him.

I was living a life of sin and I didn't even know what I was doing. I lived this way day after day, never thinking that there was anything wrong with my lifestyle. I created a blind spot to how wickedly obstinate I was until one day the Lord graciously opened my eyes.

One day, toward the later part of the year, the Holy Spirit told me to open my journal and review everything that He told me in prayer for the whole year. I cleared my schedule and began scrolling through my notes.

My dismay began quickly in the month of January. "Wow! I'm disobedient," I said to myself as I thoroughly combed through my prophetic journals. The number of incomplete instructions was overwhelming. The number of ancillary operations that I neglected were innumerable.

I wasn't lying, I wasn't sleeping around, I wasn't prayerless, but I was quite disobedient.
Day by day, I had recorded the Words I received from the Lord in prayer and I was shaken by my inaction and indecision.

I learned from that heartbreaking day that waiting on the Lord means nothing if I don't do what He says when He finally answers. In my reflection, I realized that there was no point in writing down what the Holy Spirit tells me if I didn't intend to reflect and review.

As we've discussed, revelatory people are some of the most brilliant procrastinators. Our gifts give us an edge until God's corrective measures orient us back into the reality that the gifts of the Holy Spirit are not here to make up for poor preparation.

I believe the cure for cancer, the answer to the world's climate crisis, and the advice that presidents and prime ministers long for, are sitting in someone's dusty prayer journal. We hear from God so much that we've become used to the Holy Spirit speaking to us.

Our casual approach to the knowledge of God is deceitful because we begin to think that we're in a place that we're not. We get frustrated because it seems like prophecies spoken over us haven't come to pass. We get annoyed at God because things are still the same.

The reality is that God is more frustrated than we are. We've trapped God's movement by our inaction. We want God to move for us, but He wants us to move for Him. We persist as if we have arrived at the place that He spoke of and complain in the moments where we clearly see that we have not.

This prophetic, yet fleshly, frustration stems in part from our unwillingness to actually take prophecy seriously. We get excited about what God says, but sometimes we don't even write down what God told us.

One of the major reasons why our lives remain fruitless is because we don't regularly review what God has said. In a haste to get more from God and to give more to others, we neglect to hold onto what the Lord has already spoken.

As we continue to hear from God so often in the restoration of the apostolic and prophetic in the modern church, we should learn from the Prophets of scripture.

The Prophets of the Bible would have scribes responsible for writing down the prophetic utterances that flowed from their mouths. The living water had to be inscribed on a motionless document so that the waters of Heaven could flow and spring forth to every reader and hearer.

The writers of the gospels thought that Jesus' life and ministry were so important that many of His words, deeds, and miracles were recorded for the age to come. Luke even thought that the Acts of the Apostles was critical for the reflection and memory of the church, so he wrote down the history that he lived. Peter was no different.

And I will make every effort to see that after my departure you will always be able to remember these things. -2 Peter 1:15

The Apostle Peter knew his time was short, so he wrote down some instructions before his death. This was so important to him that he made every effort to make sure that what God gave him would be available to the people.

The Bible we read was penned from a lineage aimed at preserving God's Word so that the generations ahead would know what God expects from His people. The servants of the Bible had such a reverence for keeping God's commandments that they wrote down what He said.

In today's age, we need a revival, not just of signs and wonders, but of writing down the prophetic utterances of God's generals. Not only do we need to write down the prophetic mysteries from preachers and teachers, but we also need to write down what God is saying to us directly.

How dishonorable is it to God for Him to speak to us, and we don't even value what He said enough to write it down. In our ego, we have tricked ourselves into believing that we have the ability in our finite human capacity to remember everything the God of Heaven has told us to do.

It's human nature to remember things that excite us or things that relate to our personal desires. Not everything that the Lord says to us is going to be exhilarating. We have to embrace His corrections, warnings, and futuristic references that don't make sense at the moment.

The only way to take care of God's Word is to write down and reflect upon what He has said. The direction that we need in the present season was given in a prior season. We have ready access to the instructions that the Lord expects us to fulfill.

Many prophetic Words haven't been released, books haven't been written, and businesses haven't launched because we neglected to write down and follow through on what God said yesterday. We act as if the busyness of life and the weight of our responsibilities have no chance in causing us to forget what God said to us.

On the other hand, many of us do write down what

the Lord told us to do.

The problem is how many of us actually regularly review and revisit the insight that the Holy Spirit gives us in prayer. If the Words that we get truly come from God, why do we treat God's Word like a Facebook news feed?

Our prayer journals become filled mounds of content and information that we never engage with again. God gives us daily bread, but we don't give Him a daily response in our lives. Many of the questions and concerns that we pray about are already answered in our prayer journals.

The answer to today's prayers are found in obedience to what God said yesterday. We must revisit the oracle of the Lord or face the dangers of missed opportunities and lingering disobedience.

Those that do not revisit what God has spoken unintentionally revise the path for their lives. Those that do not take the time to reflect on the promises of God will end up renouncing the promise.

Many of us live under the delusion that purpose can be passively fulfilled. We live like merely existing equates to completing the assignment that God placed us on Earth for. Our misguided assumptions will certainly be exposed on judgement day because, as Paul remarked in 1 Corinthians 3, on judgement day our works will be tested with the fire of God.

For this reason, I pray daily for the mercy of God for myself and for those that I serve. The fact that there's a judgment implies that we must intend to finish our assignment. God isn't going to wave a magic wand. Christ has already done the toughest part for us by dying on the cross so that we can have the opportunity to live for God in the first place.

A fundamental reason that many believers don't complete their God given assignments is because they don't manage tasks well. The main reasons tasks remain incomplete or poorly executed is because spiritual people assume that no planning is necessary.

We are a people so prophetically motivated that we devalue natural necessities. The word "supernatural" implies that God's super is going to shift the natural. This, however, does not mean the "natural" is not required. If there was no natural, there would be nothing for the "super" to operate on.

Planning is one of the natural tasks that we neglect because we think the fact that God is speaking means that preparation is not required on our part. While God certainly does do miraculous wonders that do not require our strict attention, there are far more examples of God speaking, followed by men and women deliberately acting out what He said.

When they obeyed God in natural tasks like picking up a staff or laying their natural hands on people,

God's supernatural power filled in the gap between what they could do and what God could do. Let's take Joseph for example:

"33 Now therefore let Pharaoh select a discerning and wise man, and set him over the land of Egypt. 34 Let Pharaoh proceed to appoint overseers over the land and take one-fifth of the produce of the land of Egypt during the seven plentiful years. 35 And let them gather all the food of these good years that are coming and store up grain under the authority of Pharaoh for food in the cities, and let them keep it. 36 That food shall be a reserve for the land against the seven years of famine that are to occur in the land of Egypt, so that the land may not perish through the famine." -Genesis 41:33-36

We often teach that Joseph only rose from the pit to the palace because of his supernatural gift of dream interpretation. However, his breakthrough also came because of his ability to develop a strategy and execute it according to what God showed him in the spirit.

While his gift did give him Pharaoh's ear, God also gave Joseph divinely inspired wisdom that made room for him in Pharaoh's palace. Joseph knew that this prophecy was useless without a strategy.

Joseph provided specific organizational structures, management systems, and a quantitative process to prepare for what was coming. A lot of us have prophecies with no plan. If Joseph would have given the prophetic Word only without a plan, the famine may have overtaken Egypt and the surrounding region.

God wasn't going to stop the drought because the people didn't prepare; it was coming regardless. God protected His people by giving them revelation, and it's our job to systematically use the revelation of the Holy Spirit to our advantage. By having a plan, Joseph not only saved much of the Earth, but he preserved the lineage and nation of the Messiah. Without a plan, procrastination is easy to access and failure is imminent.

Because of Joseph's divinely inspired strategic planning, Egypt becomes the nexus for protecting and preserving the nation of the Lord Jesus Christ. Prophecy is great, but a plan inspired by prophecy will bring us into divine alignment with what has been spoken. We have to pull on God for the plan attached to His Word.

Now what we see in the history of Joseph is an example of God foretelling future events that will happen with or without our agreement. While prophecies that release God's divine plan and judgements are critical to prepare for the future, we cannot live on these types of Words alone. We need to know how to respond to what God is saying.

Most of the time, when God speaks to us, His revelation ultimately comes in the form of instructions. We receive instructions and divine ordinances to build things that will prepare us for future seasons.

In this season, God is asking His people, "What will you build with the instructions that I gave you?"

God instructed Noah to build an ark to prepare for the season of massive flooding on the face of the Earth. Noah, having free will, had the option to comply or not with God's instructions. In this case, Noah knew that God wanted him to build the ark because destruction was coming.

There are times however, where God will simply give us instructions to execute without giving us many details. Even though these directions are very much for the present, they point to a future season. God reveals in the present to prepare for the future.

From what the scriptures reveal about Noah, we know that he had a family which implies that during this season of his life, he would have familial obligations. We also know that Noah had a physical body, which means that he had to do things like gather food, eat, and sleep. We know then that it was not possible for him to spend all twenty-four hours of the day building the ark, but the ark was completed.

The Bible does not give details on Noah's daily schedule but we can infer that in order for him to manage physical demands and potential familial obligations, he had to have some form of plan in place to balance his time to get God's work done. His plan also had to be structured in a way that would allow him to be healthy enough to do the work. Regardless of what God calls us to build, we have to have a specific and actionable plan on when and how we are going to manifest the prophetic instructions that God releases to us. Without a plan to carry out God's instructions, they often end up on the backburner.

One of the most critical elements of a plan is the deadline. We assume that because our directions come from God, we would be carnal by placing time constraints in what He's instructed us to do, but that assumption is faulty. Ecclesiastes 3:1 lets us know that "For everything there is a season, and a time for every matter under heaven."

When God gives us instructions, they are time sensitive. Even when we look at the natural order of the Earth, the sun doesn't pop up in random spurts throughout the day and the autumn leaves don't arrive in the scorching heat of the summer. There is timing for everything that God gives us.

To avoid setting dates and deadlines is to be outside of the creative order of God. Many people don't know what season an instruction should be completed by because they simply never asked the Holy Spirit. Some launch projects prematurely, while others complete their work after the season is over. We must allow the Holy Spirit to share with us what season He expects something to be completed by.

If God doesn't speak a specific season or date, that may imply that God can demand the fruit from us at any moment. We need to set a realistic deadline to follow through on what He has spoken so that we can be ready to produce at the drop of a dime.

When the Spirit of the Lord was rebuking me for not having completed this book, He stressed how I always skirted setting a deadline to finish it by. Then, He said to me that the people of God refuse to set deadlines so that they can make space for procrastination.

I was in awe. I never thought that as I was avoiding setting a hard deadline, I was actually giving myself the opportunity to let busyness and other excuses give me space to procrastinate. From that moment, I decided to prosper.

I set a deadline and I was going to get it done. When speaking to my friend Grant, I said I hope to finish by a particular date, but God used him to correct me. He cautioned me not to hope, but to make a full commitment to a particular time. In obeying God's correction, I set a deadline for completion and adjusted my schedule accordingly.

God didn't give me a specific day to be done by, but I chose the one that made sense for the season. Sometimes God gives us a task and expects us to do the planning and schedulistic changes in our lives that will bring the assignments to fruition in an expedient and effective manner.

When there is no deadline, we have not made God's

commandments a priority. Instead, His Word is merely a hobby to us. A deadline gives us a place to aim. With no deadline, a project or task may continue indefinitely.

I've seen people carry on projects that God gave them to complete for years. Without a deadline to aim at, it can go on 5 years, 10 years, or even follow us to our graves.

This realm of discipline may require sitting down to reflect upon our schedules before a new week begins. We also must identify when we're going to work on what the Lord spoke to us and for how long.

When we take the time to review our schedules ahead of the week, we have the ability to set realistic expectations for the week ahead. Another common reason that believers do not set deadlines for assignments from God is because they set unrealistic expectations of themselves.

We try deadlines and we don't meet them, so we end up just living a laissez-faire attitude toward what Christ has commissioned us to do on Earth. Failure is not an excuse to remain in dysfunctional habits.

Many deadlines are unmet simply because the deadline was not realistic in the first place. The unrealistic expectations cause deep anxiety, which discourages us from progress. We say things like "Everytime I set a deadline, I fail anyway." We shouldn't look at goals or deadlines as determinants for our character or self esteem. If we miss the mark we simply need to reflect, review, and adjust.

We must set realistic deadlines by reviewing our schedules before a new week or a new day begins. That way, we can set a plan that works for us. God knows that we have full-time jobs, families, and other ministries.

If we're not in full-time ministry, He's not expecting us to spend 8-10 hours daily launching a new endeavor. He does, however, expect us to use the time we have wisely. When we procrastinate in our daily lives, we'll likely procrastinate in the context of our purpose. If you are a prophetic person and you believe that you have a purpose aimed to reach the masses or the millions you should not wait until a week arrives to plan the week.

Busy prophetic people shouldn't wait until a new day to figure out what it should look like. We should always use today to plan for tomorrow.

Even then, when we miss a deadline that we set with careful consideration that's ok. We simply need to reflect and evaluate accordingly. There may be unexpected opportunities and events that need our attention. In some cases, we won't know the time required to complete a task until we are more deeply immersed in it. Adjustments will happen and there should be no shame or guilt in us for shifting where necessary.

A major reason that we often set poor, overly ambitious deadlines is that many of us are led by the spirit of error and not by the Spirit of God. After the Holy Spirit speaks, we move according to excitement. As we consciously or even subconsciously rush toward the finish line, we ignore the intricate details that need to be addressed.

We also ignore our human needs of rest and relaxation. Consequently, we crash. The more we rush, the more we'll miss, and the more we'll burn out. I've had to discipline myself in planning to even make space for how much rest I will need in order to be effective at what God calls me to do.

Not only are we increasing the potential to burn out, but we're also opening ourselves up to more errors when we rush because we're excited. It's ok for us to be joyful, but let's maintain the sobriety of Christ with our joy so that we can be fruitful.

All in all, God is not offended by our commitment to planning. He's not going to lift His hand from us because we have structure and deadlines. God has a way of leading us to create the structure necessary to bring forth His will.

6 STRUCTURE

It was a busy season for me. Pressures were mounting from innumerable directions. I was taking care of any and everything else except myself. In my haste, I threw all my dress shirts into a large plastic bag and threw them in the car. I got on the road and made my long, arduous morning commute. By evening I was beat, and I put off going to the dry cleaners.

While this may not seem like a big deal, I continued to do the same thing for several weeks. Every day I looked at this large black plastic bag filled with shirts that I would soon need, and I told myself I would do it later.

After weeks of procrastination, later finally came one day. I pushed myself to not take care of the many obligations of that season without dropping off these clothes.

I pulled up to my cleaners, and I found it odd that there were no other cars outside. When I got to the door, there was a note with a date for the last day to pick up clothes. In the weeks since I had last picked up some clothes, the business had shutdown.

I drove over to another cleaners. It seemed pretty awkward walking in because the whole place was silent. It's odd in the rural South to walk in a place and to not be greeted. I pushed past the seemingly loveless atmosphere as I proceeded toward the counter.

I organized my clothes, suits, shirts, and pants all in separate piles on the counter. The woman at the counter gave me a ticket and a pick-up date and quickly rescinded it. To my chagrin, she said they would actually need more time to clean my clothes because mildew had grown on some of my jackets.

I waited so long to handle my affairs that mildew grew on them. Once again, I saw another area in my life where procrastination had to die. There are tasks in our lives, that when left undone, give way to unintended growths.

There are ultimately prophetic Words that God has spoken that we've neglected, overlooked, or even forgotten. Now, we have to deal with the mildew and mold that has grown on what God has spoken.

If we don't go with what God said, something else will grow. The lack of systemic management of what Jesus has called us to do is a hindrance to the purpose of God being fulfilled in our lives.

Our management of God's purpose is unstructured, undisciplined, and wasteful. Without the proper systems, we pursue God's plan in disruptive disorder.

Systems are an important part of the life of a believer. Our spirituality makes us believe that systems are demonic. We live in a culture that hates to be under authority or apart of a system.

The Holy Spirit is like the wind. His movements are seemingly unpredictable. Although He is a free flowing Spirit, He is also a Spirit of systemic order. When observing nature, there seems to be nothing within His handiwork that exists outside of a system.

The sun rises in the East and sets in the West every day. The moon has a pre-ordained cycle. Our bodies have eleven major organ systems. Everything in His created order operates in systems. The Spirit of God is, therefore, the Spirit of the systemic.

When we fight against the proper systems in our lives, we fight against having God ordained order. Where there is no order, there will always be chaos. God often speaks or moves in ways we perceive to be random. In actuality, these seemingly erratic motions of the Holy Ghost ultimately manifest in systems of order, not chaos.

Unfortunately, we use the unpredictability of the Holy Spirit as an excuse for being undisciplined. We cannot be disciples while being undisciplined. We need to make sure that we have systems in our lives that allow us to be in divine order.

A lot of us are functionally dysfunctional. We have poor habits that we rely on our gifts to make up for. Our giftings can only take us but so far because access to a better future requires better habits. Our visionary goals and ideas are powerful, but we can't reap sustained success when our systems, planning, and strategy are poor.

We know the Holy Spirit is a planner because He speaks years ahead and He shows the end of the thing from the beginning. God speaks ahead of time, not so we can simply be excited, but so we can truly think through and plan what we need to do.

We need to consider how we need to change and adapt. God wants us to focus on how we can pull our teams together to make the necessary adjustments. He finds pleasure when we prepare by creating the proper systems that will help us have longevity in what He's showing us about the future.

We assume that because God has an unpredictable flow, often, that means that He cannot be systemic and we shouldn't be either. We relegate system and order to the business world and not to God's kingdom. Our dangerous rejection of order hinders us from progress.

The fact of the matter is that the Holy Spirit wants us to always be in tune with His rhythm. He'd rather us be more in tune with Him than with the systems that He causes us to create.

After all, He is the author of the system of the Old Testament which had particular ordinances governing how we approach God. He is also the author of the system of the New Testament, which also has different edicts on how we approach God. He is the author of both systems, but He does not want us to love the system more than we love Him, which is why He sent Jesus.

He strategically replaces systems abruptly so that we will not be enamored by the system He created for us to abide by. For example, He let the Hebrews of the Old Testament know that the system would be done away with.

He spoke through His Prophets to let the people know that the Old Testament system was a futile and temporary preparation for a better order coming under the reign and rule of the Messiah.

The prophecies of old should have been an indicator to the Old Testament believer that they shouldn't be enamored by the systems but instead should fall in love with the God that instituted them. He also told them not to worship the sun and the moon and the stars because those are just systems. We cannot worship systems over the God that has orchestrated them.

When Jesus came on the scene as the Messiah, the Pharisees had trouble receiving this new system of life because they were in love with the old system as they rebelled against the new. The demons working in the members of the Pharisees were seeking to delay a move of God by keeping them constricted within their old ways..

When God wants to do something new, the enemy will fill open leaders with procrastinatory tactics to delay what's destined to come. The spirit of procrastination can manifest as traditional religious constraint. When the enemy is trying to delay a move of God, he arrests people in stagnant traditions to try to hinder true change for a season.

The human tendency to fall in love with the comfort of what God creates is why the current generation of believers have such a pessimistic and even suspicious attitude toward systems, orders, and structures. Our fear of restriction has led us into a perverse suspicion of order. In our effort to avoid systems that constrain the Holy Spirit, we've embraced lifestyles of disorder, which is an open door for demonic activity.

In truth, we have seen people who stifle the flow of the Holy Spirit by worshipping systems and traditions rather than Jesus. The fact that people abuse and adore systems does not negate the fact that God does operate through structure. While we ought to live for Christ above seasons and traditions, we cannot stay away from systems because we're afraid that we're not going to follow them correctly or that we're going to stifle the Holy Spirit. Demonic traditions and structures that ignore the Spirit of God should be avoided altogether. Systems that come from the heart and mind of God, however, should be embraced without fear.

Once the Holy Spirit sets a system for us to abide by, we must obey accordingly. If Jesus says that we need to fast and pray, but we think we only need to go to church, then we're not in alignment with the system that He has spoken.

We have to stick with the order of the system if we're going to have a true flow of the Holy Spirit. Some people are in the spirit of delusion because they have a rush from what they think is the Holy Spirit, but it's just their feelings. They refuse to listen to leaders who lovingly correct their pace.

Our attraction to disorder fueled by our fear of becoming another generation of traditionalists is seen clearly in how isolated the body of Christ has become. We work on our own terms and few are submitted to leadership. Even in the local church context, we have abandoned the Ephesians 4:11 order of the five-fold ministry.

Many of us don't believe that we ought to be accountable to spiritual authority, and for that reason, many ministries, businesses, and projects have been launched prematurely because they do not have the proper oversight. The ministry of the Apostle, Prophet, Teacher, Evangelist, and Pastor is here to help us even in the natural endeavors the

Lord has placed upon us to tackle.

I have become wary of people that claim they hear so often from God but are not submitted to spiritual authority. Many of these people say the Holy Spirit is speaking, but it's their own feelings. They did not allow the structure of the five-fold ministry to groom and mature their sensitivity to the Holy Spirit.

From the Old Testament to the New Testament, God always had a system and structure for leadership. God did not ordain people to be off on their own, leading themselves without accountability. If there's no accountability, God is likely not in a venture or movement being launched.

God is not going to sanction something where there is no order attached because where there is disorder, there is confusion. We know that God is not the author of confusion.

Many challenge the concept that order matters, but ultimately the proof is in the pudding. The level of fruit that we're producing is lacking because we do not have the proper systems in place to keep us focused.

Regardless of the context, we have to be systematic in our everyday lives. We have to plan as we engage with God. As children of God, we need to have real conversations with Jesus about what's coming ahead so that we can plan appropriately.

God's job is to give us vision, directions, and clarity when needed. We are responsible for implementation with His power fueling us. God expects us to build teams and have conversations on how to arrive at the prophetic destiny the King has assigned us.

Systems and structure are important for our future and destiny. If we neglect the system, we're neglecting our purpose. If we build a thing without a system, there will be no longevity. As children of the digital age, we are a people addicted to rushing.

We like to see things done quickly, but not always properly because we enjoy the deceitful high from the feeling of accomplishment more than long term stability. We have a lust for completion that causes us to ignore considerations of scale and quality. We assume that because we produce something that our efforts will be impactful.

There's no need to write a book without a marketing plan or start a ministry with no team. There has to be a structure which is a part of the mentality Jesus called us to in the gospels.

28 For which of you, desiring to build a tower, does not first sit down and count the cost, whether he has enough to complete it? 29 Otherwise, when he has laid a foundation and is not able to finish, all who see it begin to mock him, 30 saying, 'This man began to build and was not able to finish.' 31 Or what king, going out to encounter *another king in war, will not sit down first and deliberate whether he is able with ten thousand to meet him who comes against him with twenty thousand? **32** And if not, while the other is yet a great way off, he sends a delegation and asks for terms of peace.**33** So therefore, any one of you who does not renounce all that he has cannot be my disciple. -Luke 14:28-33*

When Christ commissions us to do something for his Kingdom we should be more aptly prepared than a construction manager, Earthly king, or president. We have global visions, but because of our incessant desire to finish, we neglect counting the cost. We don't consider what structures are necessary to pay for the future that God showed us.

There are many things that we can build without the proper systems in place for the sake of speed, but there are dangers to our cultural preferences. With no system, what we build stands momentarily, but loses power, structure, and eventually crumbles into irreparable dust.

Therefore, we must take our time, plan, think, look ahead, and deal diligently with the things that God has given us to do. There are systems that require our development, attention, and maintenance if we're going to build consequential things for the kingdom of God that have long term effects on the arena that we are called to.

Many of us have become so aggressively suspicious of systems that we can't even hear the Lord speaking to us about the systems that we need for our homes and families. The Holy Spirit shared with me that God has systematic structures that our homes and our families need. He also shared that such structure is needed to ease the pressures and burdens of anxiety that many of us experience. Without systems we procrastinate, which eventually leads to mental fatigue.

Much of our stress is due to the lack of order. There are some regularities that the Lord wants us to experience, but when we're hearing God speak in the domain of our day to day lives, we assume that His voice is our own thoughts.

We have trouble conceptualizing the fact that God would speak in systems and make us disciplined, diligent, and even rigorous. The habits that the Lord wants to release into our personal lives are stress relieving.

We typically aren't worried about something if it is in a reliable systemic framework. I rarely hear people worry about what day their job is going to pay them. Some people get paid every other Friday. Others on the 1st and 15th of every month. Regardless of the payment schedule, each place of employment has a payroll system.

Not too many people in a stable work environment are worried about which day they're going to pick up their check or when their direct deposit is going to hit their account. This is because they're in a system that says when you show up to work, there will be a payment on a particular day by a particular time.

If man-made systems can be stress relieving, how much more can the personal systems God gives us for our homes? God wants us to have systems that affect our families, our Bible reading, and how we deal with our purpose. God has plans for how we need to prepare for the next level as we step into our new season.

We must no longer let things linger. We must bring things into divine order and hold ourselves accountable for where God wants to take us. With God's systems, we can prosper in God's kingdom.

7 JUST THE BEGINNING

There was nothing glamorous about the place. The ceiling had spots from leaks all over, and the bathroom wasn't too encouraging to say the least. Even with all the lights on, the building seemed to have a dark and dreary look, but the light of God's Word always shined intensely.

I was hooked on the spiritual surgery I got every service. I felt like a new person every time I left that strange building. We were a small congregation of no more than ten people in a building my pastor rented out for afternoon services. I sat in reflection one Sunday after my pastor delivered a powerful and convicting sermon.

He had a fiery voice that caused me to meditate on the seriousness of God, but each Word was administered with loving care. He called me to the table in the middle of the room where he and another leader were counting the offering.

I thought he wanted me to help him count the

money, but his next few words changed the rest of my life. "God said he wants you to preach next Sunday, so prepare a sermon," he said ever so calmly.

Even though I was only 14 years old, I wasn't surprised one bit. I responded with a simple ok and a nod. My pastor opened my eyes to the fact that God had been speaking to me for quite some time.

During the previous weeks, I kept having strange mental images of myself preaching. Everywhere I went, the pictures would pop into my head. It was almost as if there was no escape. I couldn't stop them from coming, and while they were happening, I wasn't in any control of what I was seeing. My only escape was ignoring them. After all, I didn't want to be that crazy guy who made up the idea that he was called to preach.

I always thought that a call to ministry was nothing to be taken lightly. I felt as if one couldn't and shouldn't just call themselves into spiritual leadership out of fanciful desire. I conveniently convinced myself that I was somehow making those images happen and that there was no need for me to align with the urgency I sensed within myself to preach.

While a person shouldn't call themselves into the responsibility of shepherding God's people, my pastor showed me that I was wrong about the origin of what was going on in my head.

God was preparing me for what was to come the

entire time. The inner urgency and the visions I was having were from God. Before those visions about preaching, I had never even thought of entering into ministry.

It was at this point that I began to trust the inner witness bubbling inside of me. I realized the soft voice that gave me comfort, direction, and assurance was indeed the Spirit of God and not just a "gut feeling." So I went home, and over the course of that week, I prepared my first sermon. I remember it like it was yesterday.

The next Sunday, I taught "The Rights and Responsibilities of a Kingdom Citizen." The congregation thought I was going to teach a mini-lesson, but God gave me a full-length sermon to deliver.

As I reflect, I realize something that I didn't know then. I was a naive, innocent, and young procrastinator. God was showing me something, but I let fear dictate my response. There are a lot of times where God is speaking to us, but we respond out of deeply ingrained fear. Because I didn't think God would call me to do such a thing, I assumed that what I saw was simply my imagination.

I didn't really seek God for clarity and I didn't ask anyone for help. I just ignored the information that was being presented to me. I thank God for His grace. I didn't know any better at the time. I had nowhere near the clarity and vision that I have now. Like my former self, some of us feel like God is leading us in a particular direction, but we are unsure.

Instead of truly allowing Him to deal with us about what we think He may be saying, we pretend we never sensed anything, or we just live in uncertainty. The problem is, the longer we wait in insecurity, the more time we have to convince ourselves out of what God is saying. The more time we waste, the more we miracles we miss.

Many of us don't move because we haven't received the confirmation that we need. At the same time, we never actively seek out support in God's Word or His people. We may ask Him passively, but how often do we seek Him? Seeking requires hunger, desperation, and a determination that is unwilling to succumb to any obstacle. Hunger says that when studying the Bible doesn't bring the answer, I'll pray.

If praying doesn't bring the answer, I'll phone a friend. If my friend can't help, I'll meet with my pastor. If my pastor can't help, then it's time to go deeper in prayer until I get a breakthrough no matter how long God takes to respond.

Hunger is a gasoline that fuels a passionate and fiery search. I once heard Pastor Michael Todd say that if you lose your keys, you're not going to just look around for them, you're going to search for them.

Our keys provide access to critical things that we can't enter into without them. We value our car keys because we need access to transportation, so we'll drop everything to find them.

We'll flip over couch cushions and look under the bed. A simple look is a very passive action, but a drastic search is more active. When we search for something, we move far outside of our comfort zone. We fear to search for the truth because the search often puts us outside of our comfort zone.

Confusion feels uncomfortable, but our culture has normalized it. Sometimes we feel good about not knowing what God really means about a particular matter. We feel safe knowing that we're close enough to Jesus to see Him, but just far enough that He can't change us too much.

The convenience of confusion that artificially calms our hunger pains for clarity. We kill our desire to investigate and pursue the deeper things of God because going deeper requires closeness. Closeness with Jesus means we have to acknowledge what He's showing us.

We live in a place where God can only take us out on the boat, but we refuse to even entertain the thought of walking on water. There's a realm of clarity that only comes when we're willing to drop everything to find the answer.

Procrastinators are not just those who hear and respond on their own schedule. They are those who are unwilling to seek God for clarity on what He's really saying. The more dependent we become on God's voice in our everyday lives, the more we will begin to hear from Him.

Those who are insensitive to the nudges of God have assignments piling up on their spiritual desks. Their supernatural voicemails are full and they have more missed appointments than they realize. To be comfortable in ignorance is to be comfortable in death.

Comfort birthed from fear places limits on our faith. Like a leash on a dog, we can only go so far when we try to follow the God of the cross with a casual approach. We pretend that we don't know God wants more because we're afraid of the consequences of obeying Him.

Maybe God might call us to do something beyond what we believe we're capable of doing or maybe God's plan will require us to give up things that we'd rather keep. So, instead of acknowledging and affirming what God is saying to us, we instead rationalize ourselves out of the divine ordinances that flow from Heaven.

When fear overrides the Word of the Lord, we rely on Earthly logic to determine whether God's will can be trusted to stand on. The problem is that 2 Corinthians 5:7 tells us that we are to walk by faith and not by sight.

When Peter walked on the water, the miracle occurred as long as he walked by faith. As soon as he began to walk by sight, he sank. When our logic causes us to fail, we will see that God knows far more than we do.

That's why the Apostle Paul told us in 1 Corinthians 1:27 that God chooses the foolish things of the world to confound the wise. When we walk in our own wisdom, we become foolish, and God has to humble us. However, when we choose to humble ourselves, by submitting to God's Word, which may appear to be foolish, He will make us wise.

Paul experienced this scripture first hand. He was comfortable murdering and imprisoning Christians until one day while he was on the road to Damascus, Jesus quite literally knocked him off of his high horse in Acts 9.

When God wants someone to step out of their comfort zone, He interrupts them to make them submit to what He'd been saying the whole time. Sometimes the interruption is simple like my pastor telling me to preach next Sunday. Other times, God may take more traumatic measures like what He did with Paul.

After Jesus appears to him and intercepts him into ministry, he was blind for three days. Before Paul was walking by what he could see, but afterwards he had to live with darkness over his eyes.

When we become comfortable living a certain way, believing a certain way, and thinking a certain way,

God's light blinds us so that we can learn to walk by faith and not by sight.

Interruptions are the inheritance of the disciples of Christ. God constantly grooms us to close our eyes and expand our faith. The more of God that we want to see, the less we'll be able to use our eyes.

Prayer

Lord, help me to recognize when you are speaking. Forgive me for any time when you were impressing, revealing, speaking, or showing me something and I ignored you by simply going about my day. I confess that there have been times when my heart has been hardened toward your voice, and I missed your Word to me. Father open my spiritual senses and give me greater clarity. Remove any spiritual blindness or ear wax clogging and blocking my sensitivity to your precious and vibrant spirit. You are a God of the living and not the dead, so Lord awaken any deadened spiritual senses. Revive and awaken any dormant gifts and callings within my spirit. Let me not confuse your voice with my own thoughts, but allow me to discern the clear separation of your distinct beautiful voice.

Homework

- Reflect on any area that you feel God calling you into and ponder about any apprehensions you may have in relation to that calling.
    - List the reasons that you are apprehensive (fears, excuses, etc.).
    - Next to each reason write a solution as to how you can overcome your apprehension.
    - Choose the greatest apprehension that you list and do a topical Bible study on it (i.e., if fear of failure was your greatest issue, then you should study fear).

8 WIT AND WISDOM

I sat a bit bewildered as everyone in the room cheered on. I suppose that's not uncommon for me because I typically see things differently than a lot of people around me. I really don't try to be so different, but that's just the way I am.

There's always a part of me that wants to feel guilty for thinking differently, and that day was a perfect example. I looked around at the entire well-lit room. Almost everyone was either standing in adulation or sitting in joyous agreement.

I, however, couldn't find an ounce of energy to put on a fake smile. My jaws tightened and, as typical within a frustrating moment, there seemed to be a weight on my chest. Not a heavy one, but it's just something that sat there for a few moments.

I was really confused as to why everyone was so excited about a comment that seemed so weak to me. I was at a political forum on faith and politics, which we seem to have a lot of in the South.

While discussing gun violence and school shootings, someone commented that the problem is that we don't pray in schools anymore.

Here's a disclaimer before I proceed, I definitely do think prayer in schools is great. I'm a man of much prayer who's heavily involved in the school system, which gives me ample opportunity to pray with my students often. My students know me for prophecy, word of knowledge, and having a full-on deliverance ministry right on campus. I grieve and pray for families who have to deal with such an unbearable loss regularly.

Now with that being said, although everyone else was thrilled, I found the remarks on prayer as shallow and underwhelming. From my perspective, the comments reflected a vast oversimplification of complex socio-economic issues ranging from mental health awareness to economic policy.

What made things worse to me was that none of the candidates on the forum had ever proposed any legislation or launched any political movements to bring public prayer back to schools. The candidates didn't challenge the saints to call their legislators and never even cited the landmark case that took prayer from schools, Engel v. Vitale.

I knew some of the people in the audience, and they were active in their churches, but politically unawakened. They didn't know who their legislators were, which means they never call them, and they're typically unaware of what's happening in the world outside of the four walls of the church.

I saw the candidates call to get prayer back in schools with no follow through or accountability as nothing more than a doctor trying to prescribe Tylenol to cure stage 4 cancer.

The super, with no natural, isn't going to get things done on Earth. The church has been using prayer to feel better about their inaction. We're praying for God to do things that we need our legislators to do, but we never even ask them. We've allowed prayer to make us lazy and fruitless in a world filled with emergencies.

15 If a brother or sister is poorly clothed and lacking in daily food, 16 and one of you says to them, "Go in peace, be warmed and filled," without giving them the things needed for the body, what good is that? 17 So also faith by itself, if it does not have works, is dead. -James 2:15-17

To pray for legislative action, but to be politically silent, is an example of our faith without works culture. God is not going to simply change everything because we ask Him to or have faith that He can. He's not going to sow into our laziness and ignorance.

In the days of the old, the Prophets would lead the nation by counseling the King. However, in today's climate, Prophets are content with not knowing who their senators are. Prophets are impacting a church culture that is comfortable with having no impact on the world. For this reason, the world thinks that the church is crazy.

There are miracles, signs, and wonders, that haven't occurred because we're so busy focusing on growing our churches that we don't have time to be in the world. Presidents and politicians don't get to see the miraculous. CEOs remain agnostic because we're unwilling to put works with our faith. We pray for world change instead of investing the knowledge necessary to become change agents.

One of the major impediments to the forward motion of the body of Christ is the severe lack of natural knowledge. We know the sixty-six books of the Bible well, but lack knowledge and wisdom of natural concepts that help further us in the cause of God.

We have come to be supernatural geniuses, but we seem to lack common sense. There are many so-called Prophets to the nations and Governmental Apostles who don't even have passports.

Oddly enough the Prophets to city hall, county council, the state house, and congress are nowhere to be found. The prophetic movement is absent when it comes to speaking to the powers that handle the political affairs that affect our daily lives in the local context, let alone international relations.

God is not the only force that influences what happens on Earth. Genesis says that He gave mankind dominion over the Earth. While He may set up and sit down political and economic leaders, He sets the tone, and they must follow through. How can unsaved political leaders know what the tone should be if they've never heard His voice through His servants? The gift of prophecy once known for touching the hearts of kings is now selfishly boxed up for personal life application, church growth, and nothing more.

The question is then, how do we come out of the church and begin to spread the gospel in other spheres of influence? As Paul wrote, we must become "all things to all men." There are mission fields in the world that we have not tapped into because we've been so focused on spiritual growth that we've let the natural decay.

45 Thus it is written, "The first man Adam became a living being"; the last Adam became a life-giving spirit. 46 But it is not the spiritual that is first but the natural, and then the spiritual. -1 Corinthians 15:45-46

Our doctrines and teachings, even across denominational lines, have created a Christianity that sees the natural as unnecessary. We focus so much on the spirit that the natural is an afterthought, where in reality, the Word of God lets us know that it was the natural that preceded the spiritual.

This principle is important for every Christian entrepreneur, author, church planter, or business owner looking for God to bring increase. We do not see the level of fruit that we want because we are trying to get God to breathe on projects that don't have bodies.

Wisdom, knowledge, and understanding as a unit are the body that God wants to breathe on. Essentially, we want God to impart to visions that we refuse to obtain natural knowledge on. We want Him to make our companies skyrocket, but we don't want to read books that will help us manage our employees better.

We lust for God to promote us in our endeavors, but we refuse to get an understanding of what we're called to do. God said, let there be light, but there was already an Earth for God to bring light to.

If we want to see God enlighten our endeavors, we must assume the position and posture of education. Without wisdom, we will always be underprepared. There are some instructions from God that will only come when we have the requisite knowledge to understand. The Lord isn't going to give us keys to stock market success if we never learn investing basics.

One of the most concerning manifestations of the spirit of procrastination in God's church is most visible after a prophetic Word is released. We think we're waiting on God, but we're missing momentum.

God prophecies entrepreneurship, but we never think to read a book on business. The Lord tells us that we're going to own properties, but we never think to speak with someone who owns real estate to ask them questions about best practices.

It seems that when God speaks, we believe that getting wisdom and understanding of what He has spoken is unnecessary. The acquisition of wisdom is a key to walk in purpose. Procrastination in preparation will lock up the skill power of the future. Some prophecies will be unlocked when our education status and credentials align with what God promised. God's Word is a sign of what we should be preparing for, not idly waiting for.

A life that lacks required wisdom for the next instruction from God is a life lived out of season. Many of us are like apples that bloom in the winter only to be destroyed by the freezing temperature. An out of season life is always frustrated by unfulfilled prophecies.

Many of us receive prophecies that we neglect to prepare for. The prophetic isn't just showing us what to do, but what to study. We need to get wit and wisdom before the season of fulfillment arrives, or we will not be able to maintain the promises of God.

Many of us constrict and constrain the magnitude of what God is willing to bless us with because we refuse to mentally prepare. We act as if our brain is demonic and reading will bring us to our demise.

Prophetic people seem to only define one realm of sensitivity. That is the realm where we hear from God. There is, however, another dimension of sensitivity that awakens when we obey God.

Many people hear from God and see visions but do not follow through on the instructions that God gives. Those that are truly sensitive to the Holy Spirit master hearing from Him on a rare level by immediately preparing according to what He shows us about the seasons ahead. The insensitive will be ineffective. Proverbs 4:7 gives us instructions that apply to almost every prophetic Word that we receive.

Wisdom is the principal thing; therefore get wisdom: and with all thy getting get understanding. -Proverbs 4:7

Whenever God speaks about the future, our immediate action should be to get wisdom and understanding. The fact of the matter is that the scripture says with "all" of our getting we should get understanding.

There are books, articles, relational expertise, and other mediums of wisdom connected to everything that proceeds out of the mouth of God. Our lack of preparation for the future shows that either we are not serious about what God says or we don't believe Him.

If we lived this scripture as often as we quote it, the world wouldn't be able to contain the miracles and mighty moves of God that would manifest. I also believe that we would see more people from all types of backgrounds be transformed by the power of God..

We've relegated the principles of reaping and sowing only to our financial benefit. If we want to reap bigger returns in the realm of our purpose, we have to do a better job of sowing into what God has declared over us.

We have come to an age where we have great understanding of prayer, fasting, and reading the Word, but we are in a self-inflicted drought of wisdom and understanding. Some of the wisdom we need is simply common sense, but for many of us, there is a realm of knowledge that we need to unlock the mysteries and hidden figures of our purpose. Proverbs 1:7 is another popular verse that shows us how mentally sedentary the church has become.

The fear of the Lord is the beginning of knowledge; fools despise wisdom and instruction. -Proverbs 1:7

We know the first part of Proverbs 1:7 intimately, but the second half is often left unquoted. The Bible describes fools as those that hate wisdom and instruction. That implies that there are many fools in the body of Christ.

We can tell what we hate, not only by what angers us but by what we avoid. Many of us hate reading, learning, and pursuing knowledge and understanding. We have developed a concerning preference for ignorance that has caused a deep stagnancy in many prophetic endeavors.

Unfortunately, we have a tendency only to study for school. We rarely study the Holy Spirit wants us to focus on. God has things for us to read and research so that we can arrive in prominence and prosperity for the difficult times coming on the Earth.

Procrastinators put off personal growth and development for the sake of the busyness of today's challenges. There is an entirely new realm of access to souls that need our ministry when we make the commitment to not just knowing about our purpose but acquiring the relevant competencies for what God has called us to do.

Some of us need to know about organizing teams, running organizations, and growing as leaders. We should know about history, advances in technology, and developments in policy. If we don't gain insight into the world that God called us to enter into, we won't be able to reach the audience that we're called to. The readers are the leaders ruling in every mountain of influence.

A common habit among today's billionaires is the acquisition of knowledge, wisdom, and understanding. There are many wicked men and women have wealth because, although they don't have Jesus, they apply Biblical principles on seeking wisdom to their lives, and they reap the benefits.

An upright example can be found in Daniel, the Old Testament statesman and Prophet, who knew well the "literature and language of the Chaldeans." Daniel had access to prophesy to King Nebuchadnezzar not only because of his prophetic acumen, but because of his mental resilience to learn and study. Our study habits will open the door for us to speak God's Word in arenas that He created for us to occupy.

The Lord spoke to me about the current political climate in the United States. He told me that when this season is over, there is going to be a void for his people to fill. He wants to see spirit filled entrepreneurs, creatives, engineers, and policymakers take charge in and fill the seats of those who have been unfaithful.

This charge from Heaven to take on such mantles requires us to speak the language of a new audience. The language of the unbeliever is often based on natural understanding. If we don't adopt the reading and learning habits to match where God is calling us to, we will continue to complain about how few believers hold positions of influence and power in the Earth.

We pray for more spirit-filled politicians and play-makers to arise, but we're unwilling to grow our mental capacities to a place where we can fill the space of a diligent and organized unbeliever. We have dishonored the gifts of the Holy Spirit by believing that His revelation is here to make up for our willful ignorance. The Lord does not bless laziness.

As Daniel did, we must be able to balance the work of the King of Kings and the kings of the Earth so that the Nebuchadnezzars of the world can begin to worship the God of all glory. Intercession alone cannot bring the change that we desire to see in the Earth. God is looking to raise up intercessors that are willing to intervene. We must master God's sixty-six book love letter to a point where we can utter his profound truths in the language of the audience that we're called to.

We think prayer and favor are here to compensate for our laziness. The reality is that prayer allows us to discern what God is favoring so we can be diligent in what He reveals.

We have reduced spiritual warfare to decrees and chants. Many of our spiritual warfare tactics are no more than mysticism, which is why nothing seems to change. Spiritual warfare has great power when what we hear in prayer comes to Earth. Jesus prayed, "Thy kingdom come. Thy will be done on Earth as it is in Heaven" and the Father led Him to act in ways that brought Heaven's will to Earth.

The Kingdom of God, however, is not just in the healing of the sick and prophecy, but in what we build. Jesus advanced the Kingdom of God by establishing a worldwide organization with a corporate headquarters in Heaven, we know it as the church.

He began it with twelve employees and has garnered a market size of 31% of the world (roughly 2.2 billion Christians if you assume everyone who says they follow Christ means so). He systematically influenced billions of people by using His executive staff of Apostles, Prophets, Teachers, Evangelists, and Pastors to plant and maintain offices in all 195 countries in the world today.

Jesus' concept for spiritual warfare was not only the casting out of devils, but the building of His church to carry out His mission. While we are filled with the Holy Spirit in Christ's church, we have natural bodies. God didn't take away our bodies and make us float around as spirits when we gave our lives to Him, which means He intends to use our bodies to build.

Christ used His Earthly body to build an organization that would carry out His mission, vision, and plan for the continued expansion of the Heavenly Kingdom which He descended from. By launching the church, He fought the power of hell in a way that outlasted His Earthly days. To do this, Jesus had to recruit, train, engage, and use many natural skills to build something that would destroy the works of the devil.

The moral of the story is that an important part of spiritual warfare is the building of organizations and the acquisition of resources. Christ's chief, but weaker adversary, the devil, copies Jesus' leadership style by creating organizations and movements to keep people bound.

Let's take the pornography industry as an example. The porn industry is a multibillion-dollar industry so powerful that some say that it's not "unrealistic to say that porn makes up 30% of the total data transferred across the internet." Not to mention, porn and human trafficking reinforce each other. "If someone contributed even one view to the 28.5 billion views of free porn online in the last year, he may have watched a victim of sex trafficking appearing under duress on camera."

The enemy is literally paying people full-time to support his mission of keeping people bound in sin. The bios of the C-level executives for the porn company Playboy are unbelievable. They all have advanced degrees from the world's most competitive universities and they've held high positions at notable fortune five hundred companies.

Through their power to hire, train, and pay Playboy is able to perform spiritual warfare on a different level. They don't bind, loose or speak in tongues to accomplish their mission. Playboy and other porn companies keep millions of addicts bound by loosing content filled with some of the most perverse imaginations of human debauchery possible.

From Playboy, we can see that capital heightens our influence in warfare. Their business was able to learn enough to acquire millions of dollars to hire highly skilled men and women to work in their ministry full-time. With a team of employees able to focus diligently, the organization was able to grow large enough to imprison the masses.

The ability to hire is a warfare tactic that helps bring people out of poverty with an intent to focus them on a particular mission and purpose. However, the enemy is using these strategies to keep people bound.

If the sons of darkness can build and grow, how much more potential is there in the sons of Light who are filled with the Spirit of the Almighty God?

The people of God can war better when we learn to war like Jesus by building something the world hasn't seen. There's a realm of spiritual warfare that can only be fought through the streams of influence. Influence is determined by what we build, and the scale of what we build is determined by what we know. An uneducated architect is never given a contract to build skyscrapers.

As saints, we have been highly reactive. We pray, bind, and loose while the world is building. As Jesus did, we must spend ample time praying and ample time moving. Some of us are called to be visionaries like Nehemiah, who led the people of God to build the wall in the city of God. Others must be the builders who stand and support new generations of Nehemiah like visionaries who are rising from obscurity.

The trouble that is everyone wants to be a Nehemiah, Moses, or Paul, but few see the importance of being an Eliashib, Aaron, or Timothy. The kingdom is having trouble advancing because few want to serve as the supporting cast to visionary leaders that have been ordained by God.

The Lord said to Moses, 2 "See, I have called by name Bezalel the son of Uri, son of Hur, of the tribe of Judah, 3 and I have filled him with the Spirit of God, with ability and intelligence, with knowledge and all craftsmanship, 4 to devise artistic designs, to work in gold, silver, and bronze, 5 in cutting stones for setting, and in carving wood, to work in every craft." -Exodus 31:1-5

What many neglect to understand is that just as God called Moses, He called and ordained Bezalel to support him. The ministry of the craftsman is just as important as the ministry of the visionary. Both are ordained by God. Without proper teams, nothing consequential can be accomplished.

An industry as wicked as porn, has recognized that every skilled staff member can't be the CEO because there must be a supporting cast to advance the will of an organization or movement in the Earth.

The immense nature of a gifting does not automatically imply that someone is called to be the senior leader of a church, apostolic movement, company, or organization. Most of us with considerable talent, need to submit what God has given us to someone else so that there can be a mega movement.

The issue of organizational structure and submission lies within the wit of the leader. A leader must know how to manage the help that God sends in a way that isn't just operational, but flowing in the order, authority, and power of God. That takes care and a sharp attention to the right details.

If a modern-day Moses was like many of us, he would have pursued wisdom that was irrelevant to his calling. He would have read books, watched courses, and consumed YouTube videos about craftsmanship rather than spending his time leading the children of Israel to the promised land.

Visionaries struggle with receiving Bezalels in their life because the devil tricks them into thinking that they have to do everything by themselves. If Nehemiah would have focused on building the wall with his own hands instead of organizing and leading teams to do so, the wall would have never been finished. A sign of an immature visionary is one who puts his hands where his eyes should be. In other words, many visionaries have a tendency to try to build things with their own hands instead of asking how they can oversee the hands of others. Vision, sight, planning, organizing, and forethought are skill sets that leaders need to focus on.

Procrastination is a consequence of an over extension of one's abilities. When we try to do everything on our own we place the core activities of our purpose on the backburner. When a visionary tries to put their hands in everything, they can't replicate themselves. It takes longer to get things done because their arms are too short to reach every part of what's being built. Teamless pioneers build slowly.

The devil's plot is to trick the visionary leader into focusing on apparent emergencies that are outside of their creative purpose. The only way for leaders to break free themselves from this scheme is to pursue wisdom that keeps them focused on the target that God has set before them. Regardless of your role, let's learn to build better as the King's children so that we can advance His mission more effectively. When we know better, we will do better.

9 INSANITY

It was a busy night in the restaurant and the waitress was totally swamped. Little did she know, a man who could change her whole life just walked in. In her haste to serve other customers, she ignored him.

Eventually, he just seated himself. He was a man of wealth and influence in the community, and Erica had been struggling to pay her debts. College tuition was out of reach, so she was working part-time to cauterize her dreams that seemed to be bleeding out.

Mr. Jones had the social and political clout to help her with getting her dream job and the type of money to pay tuition for everyone in the restaurant. He walked in that night with the intention to give his waiter or waitress a major gift for nothing in return.

This man of influence with a warm and bright personality was simply looking to have a nice simple meal before heading home. He often asked people questions and wanted to understand people's stories.

He was really into hearing the problems that others face. After all, there was a season of his life where he had to serve tables just like Erica to make ends meet. 10 minutes went by and no one took his order. As time continued to press on, he occasionally signaled to Erica. She would acknowledge him, but never came.

Mr. Jones was a man of purpose and refused to waste anymore of his time. He always felt the more time he wasted, the less time he'd have to make an impact on the lives of others. After waiting patiently, he decided to get up and leave.

Erica missed one of the biggest opportunities of her life, and she didn't even know it. Erica served everyone else except the one that was there to serve her. The relationship between Erica and Mr. Jones is no different than the type of relationship we have with God.

When we procrastinate long enough, God has to move on to someone who is available to receive what He has for them. When we serve Jesus with promptness, He will reward us.

To neglect Him, on the other hand, is to neglect the promise. Often God moves on to a new restaurant, and we don't even realize it because we're too busy paying attention to everyone else.

If we keep God waiting, the consequences may be invisible, but deadly. The progression of God's rebukes weighs heavier and heavier as we remain inactive in what God has spoken. Saul, the first king of ancient Israel in the Old Testament, learned this lesson the hard way.

22 And Samuel said, Hath the Lord as great delight in burnt offerings and sacrifices, as in obeying the voice of the Lord? Behold, to obey is better than sacrifice, and to hearken than the fat of rams. 23 For rebellion is as the sin of witchcraft, and stubbornness is as iniquity and idolatry. Because thou hast rejected the word of the Lord, he hath also rejected thee from being king. -1 Samuel 15:22-23

Saul had been given instructions from God through Samuel the Prophet to take new territory for the nation of Israel, but to destroy everything that was already in the land. Saul instead preserved some of the best things from the land, including the sheep and oxen to make sacrifices to the Lord.

God was not pleased with Saul's partial obedience and was sternly rebuked by Samuel. God wanted obedience and not sacrifice. Saul only obeyed part of God's instructions, which meant that he was ultimately disobedient.

Procrastinators are stubborn. They reject the Word of the Lord by leaving assignments incomplete. We think we're pleasing God because we've done a portion of what He asked, but God sees our willful slackness as rebellion. He sees rebellion as witchcraft. Our sacrifices to God in prayer, church, and ministerial obligations cannot make up for our wizardry.

The Bible lets us know in 1 John 3:8 that Christ came to destroy the works of the devil, and we are His disciples. Everything God tells us to do is directly attached to a work of the devil being destroyed. When we neglect to obey the Holy Spirit, we are leaving works of the devil active. God didn't take Saul's partial obedience lightly.

He got too comfortable with God and what he was called to do. He didn't think his obedience was that big of a deal. His actions showed that he thought he could do just enough to get by. Saul's just enough mentality brought the premature demise of his kingdom.

God saw Saul's disobedience as him rejecting his instructions. When we are comfortable with partial obedience, demise is just around the corner. Our comfortability is setting us up for a failure that we can't reverse.

We have the faulty assumption that our hearts will remain pure after we disobey God. However, the drug of disobedience is a captivating force that corrupts the heart. Saul shows the true posture of his heart after being rebuked by Samuel:

Then he said, "I have sinned; yet honor me now before the elders of my people and before Israel, and return with me, that I may bow before the Lord your God." -1 Samuel 15:30

Saul only wanted to keep Samuel around for personal gain. He only repented before Samuel so he could retain prestige and honor among the people, not so that he could please God. He figured that the absence of Samuel would make people less likely to keep him as a ruler, so he repented with his words, but not with his heart.

To constantly leave the commandments of God incomplete desensitizes us to the fact that the Holy Spirit who speaks to us is in fact, the very spirit of God Almighty. To become so callously brazen to the commandment of God that we believe His instructions are optional is a dangerous place to be.

There is a delusion that comes when we partially obey God. We deceive ourselves into thinking everything is ok and we get drunk with a god complex that makes us think we can obey God at our own pace. We don't have the fear of the Lord because our personal ambitions are sitting where our reverence for God should be.

It is a fearful thing to fall into the hands of the living God. -Hebrews 10:31

We know that the church has lost the fear of the Lord because procrastination seems to reign. Like Saul, what we refuse to complete will kill us in the long run. The odd thing is that Saul remained king for quite some time after God rejected him. He even had enough time to fight against his replacement, King David, for over a decade in hopes to retain power.

1 Samuel 15, was not Saul's first act of disobedience. He had a tendency to follow the voices of people rather than the voice of the Lord. In the previous chapters of this portion of the Bible, Samuel had already declared that Saul's kingdom was going to end because of his disobedience. Yet, before he died, Saul continued to stay in authority even though God wasn't pleased with him. Authority on Earth does not imply that someone has authority in Heaven.

After Samuel's initial prophetic judgment, Saul seemed to have lost his sense of security. He was secure in his position and title, but seemed to struggle mentally after God decided to revoke his authority.

The account of 1 Samuel 14 shows some very strange and erratic behavior from Saul. In the dead heat of an intense military campaign, Saul forces his army to a fast under a vow before the Lord, imposing a great burden on his warriors. His son Jonathan breaks the unreasonable fast, and he orders his execution.

Although his son survives, Saul's brazen willingness to kill his son highlights the dark headspace that he was in. After engaging with the spirit of procrastination, we can keep a God-given position, but have a demonic mindset. Just because we retain authority and power does not imply that God is pleased by our decisions.

Many gifted people walk in the power of God, but are outside of His presence. The gifts that come with our callings do not justify us before Jesus Christ.

A lifestyle of procrastination is very deceptive because our gifts still work, and we keep much of the authority that God has placed into our hands. Yet, the world has no clue what God has whispered into our ears. The planet may see greatness, but when we refuse to move at the pace that God has called us to, we're living in the depths of mediocrity.

God's people have become comfortable with mediocre obedience. We walk in our callings in a casual manner. There's a generation of Sauls in the Earth. They are pastoring churches, hosting conferences, doing revivals, and writing books. Like Saul, they believe that obeying the Holy Spirit is optional. Similar to the modern day procrastinator, Saul's trouble began when he decided to move on his timing and not God's. From that moment, he was out of sync with the move of God for the rest of his life. Eventually, he came to a place that he couldn't recover from. Many of us have been living lives as if procrastination doesn't have the power to lead us outside of the will of God. Missed opportunities, missed moments, and missed momentum will eventually cause collateral damage.

The weight of what's gone undone and incomplete in our lives begins to weigh on our psyches as time goes on. The frustration of knowing that there's more in us than what we're producing erupts into an overwhelming place. Eventually, this frustrating reality causes a cycle of inconsistency where we have exciting highs of productivity and depressing lows of inactivity.

The two-week wonder lifestyle leads to a Saul like insanity that is irrecoverable. The greatest repro-bates will be the ones that are still trying to do work for God but are unwilling to grab hold to con-sistency. In one moment, Saul wanted to do right by the Lord and in the very next he wanted to murder David.

The bipolar nature of the Saul spirit is characterized by indecision birthed from procrastination. One day we say we're going to focus on what God said to do and then the next day we live according to how we feel. One moment we choose to be secure in our identity in God, and then in the next we reject what God has called us to do because we hate the limita-tions and responsibilities it has placed upon us.

Unfortunately, those who follow Saul's behavior will have his dark end.

4 Then Saul said to his armor-bearer, "Draw your sword, and thrust me through with it, lest these un-

circumcised come and thrust me through, and mistreat me." But his armor-bearer would not, for he feared greatly. Therefore Saul took his own sword and fell upon it. 5 And when his armor-bearer saw that Saul was dead, he also fell upon his sword and died with him. 6 Thus Saul died, and his three sons, and his armor-bearer, and all his men, on the same day together. -1 Samuel 31:4-6

Saul's insanity eventually led him to take his own life. There are many suicidal people walking the Earth right now who don't intend to harm themselves. The primary aim of the spirit of suicide isn't to kill anyone. In actuality, the main objective of the spirit of suicide is to murder our purpose. The physical death of someone is just the icing on the cake.

Suicide comes to lead people into behavior that sabotages purpose. Chief manifestations of the spirit of suicide come in the form of procrastinatory habits. Procrastination causes people to delay the fulfillment of the purpose that God called them to. We assume that because God's mercy is so powerful that time is subsequently just as merciful. What God has called us to do is time sensitive.

The Lord is a God of times and seasons. Many of us never walk into the fullness of what God has called us to do because the spirit of suicide has tricked us into procrastinating so much that we're not ready when our hour arrives.

There's a specific hour that you were designed for.

To live a life where you casually mishandle your minutes is to train yourself to mishandle your hour. Our purpose requires our dedication, focus, and readiness. Don't be so distracted by how you feel now that you're unable to walk into what's next. Saul spent decades of his life fighting the next instead of repenting and submitting to it.

One of the most startling things about Saul's death is that his armor bearer died with him. If we continue with suicidal habits, those who are following us will end their lives prematurely just like us.

The spirit of death is released indiscriminately when we refuse to complete what God called us to. Not only does suicide want to kill our purpose, but that of everyone that we're connected to and every one that we're assigned to.

Many Sauls are roaming the Earth right now. They lead, launch businesses, host conferences, and write books, but live in mediocrity. They're surviving, but procrastination and inconsistency have gripped them to a place where the world never sees what God wanted to use them to release into the Earth.

They release people into the generational curse of incomplete assignments. Their spiritual offspring are birthed into the same habits, mindsets, personal limitations, and excuses that held back the prior generation. Without the power of God and a deep personal revelation from Jesus Christ, the next generation will continue to live according to self-imposed and demonically stirred limits rather than the glory and promises of God Almighty.

Procrastination kills the future. We must all consider the generational effects of poor habits. Such consideration is especially essential for every minister, business leader, and disciple maker. However, the relevance of this lesson transcends traditional leadership. We are all leaders because we all have influence. Whether we realize it or not, there's always someone watching us. Even if we're not the star of the show, our energy, attitude, effort, and focus are nonverbal instructions on how to live. We must make a commitment to God to finish the works that He called us to start so that future generations can pioneer the solutions the world has yet to see.

ABOUT THE AUTHOR

Eddie Massey III is a Pastor and social entrepreneur with a passion for helping people live like Christ. He's been preaching since the age of 14 and aims to raise a generation of prophetic people that will not only hear God's Word, but become the truth that they read. He serves as an Associate Pastor at the Feast of the Lord church in South Carolina. He also runs a mission organization called Fresh Foundation, which trains believers of all backgrounds in prophetic evangelism.

freshfoundation.org